DRAWN
TO THE
DIVINE

DRAWN TO THE DIVINE

A Spirituality of Revelation

WILLIAM E. REISER, S.J.

AVE MARIA PRESS
Notre Dame, IN 46556

Imprimi potest

Very Rev. Robert E. Manning, S.J., Provincial
Society of Jesus of New England

Permissions:

All Scripture quotations in this publication are from the Holy Bible, New
International Version. Copyright © 1973, 1978, 1984, International Bible
Society.

Quotations from *The Documents of Vatican II,* Abbott-Gallagher edition, are
reprinted with permission of America Press, Inc., 106 West 56th Street, New
York, NY 10019. © 1966. All Rights Reserved.

"We Are Only Ourselves" from *Audubon: A Vision.* Copyright © 1969 by Robert
Penn Warren. Reprinted from *New and Selected Poems 1923-1985* by Robert Penn
Warren, by permission of Random House, Inc.

Quotation from SUMMA CONTRA GENTILES *Book One: God* translated by Anton
C. Pegis, F.R.S.C. © 1955 by Doubleday & Company, Inc.

Library of Congress Catalog Card Number: 87-71431

International Standard Book Number: 0-87793-376-7

Cover design: Elizabeth J. French

Printed and bound in the United States of America.

Contents

Then the man and his wife heard the sound of the LORD God as he was walking in the garden in the cool of the day, and they hid from the LORD God among the trees of the garden. But the LORD God called to the man, "Where are you?"

He answered, "I heard you in the garden, and I was afraid because I was naked; so I hid."

—Genesis 3:8-10

> I opened for my lover,
> but my lover had left; he was gone.
> My heart had gone out to him when he spoke.
> I looked for him but did not find him.
> I called him but he did not answer.
>
> —Song of Songs 5:6

We never know what we have lost, or what we have found.
We are only ourselves, and that promise.
Continue to walk in the world. Yes, love it!

—Robert Penn Warren

A Personal Foreword

My earliest recollection of being in church was not my earliest memory of experiencing the presence of God. Whatever sense of God's presence I acquired as a child did not attach to being in church but to the expansiveness of the earth and the sky, which, I realized much later, was an intuition about the connection between openness and freedom, and holiness. I had unconsciously associated the feeling of being free with the mystery of God. Yet having once experienced the holy mystery, how could I have interpreted my experience and learned about God, except through the church? My desire for God led me, eventually, to seek to be a priest. I thought that serving the church was the finest thing imaginable since the church was the place where men and women could learn about, and sometimes even touch, the holy, liberating mystery of God. All that was before Vatican II.

The Second Vatican Council precipitated a religious-cultural upheaval in my life and in the lives of many other Catholics. Do not get me wrong: I have welcomed the Council. But something I had leaned upon for years seemed to pass with the Council. That innocent, almost naive association of the divine presence with the church was lost. In my imagination the church had come to represent God's presence. It made me secure and confident about the work I envisioned myself doing some day as a priest, about what was necessary for my salvation and the salvation of others, and about what God was like. Unfortunately the sense of knowing that I was in God's presence from the feeling of being free had faded as I entered a world which was increasingly male, authoritarian and ecclesiastical. Whether this happened as a result of my own religious immaturity or as a result of the way the church had schooled us in the faith, I cannot say. In letting me become preoccupied with its own beauty and form, and, yes, in telling me too often and too surely what God expected of me, the church had fenced in my religious landscape and enclosed the divine mystery (which leads, of course, to distorting it). In any case, I forgot about the liberating, breathtaking openness and beauty of the holy mystery of God. If, after Vatican II, some disaffected voices were wondering whether people could still touch the mystery of God when they participated in the life of the church, we should have been hastening to rejoin, "But how much of that mystery had they genuinely experienced in the years prior to the Council?" Had the church, for many Catholics, inserted itself between them and God, so that they were experiencing more of the numinous element in various aspects of the church—its ritual and devotions, its liturgical practice and moral teachings, its hierarchical structure and asceticism—than the Holy Spirit of God, which ought to animate these things and which always surpasses them?

Nevertheless, more than 20 years after Vatican II, it still makes sense, and perhaps more sense than ever, to pose the question, "Do people today touch the mystery of God when they participate in the life of the church?" I believe they can, but because of the Council the perspective from which we ask the question has shifted. The church as institution is not the locus of mystery. Rather, the believing community, men and women of faith—people *of God*—is the place where the divine mystery becomes revealed. As one of my theology professors fondly and repeatedly reminded us, the principal mode of Christ's real presence in the church is his presence in the heart of the believer through faith.

Vatican II crystallized for me (and Vatican II here symbolizes a deep, dramatic reversal of my former way of conceiving the church, ministry, and God's presence in the world) the difference between being *in* church and *being* church, between institution and inner life, between external form and mystery. I readily admit that these aspects are forever intertwined. But as I hope to show in the pages which follow, the revelation of the mystery of God occurs primarily in our being church which for me (and for many others) has been a liberating and exhilarating recovery of Paul's insight expressed in his Letter to the Colossians. There Paul speaks of "the mystery that has been kept hidden for ages and generations . . . this mystery, which is Christ in you, the hope of glory" (Col 1:26-27). What is this mystery, this incomparably wonderful truth about human beings? It is nothing less than this: Men and women through their living can reveal the presence of Christ to the world.

But this is also a decidedly difficult challenge. It is deceptively easy for us to objectify the divine presence by representing the church as a mystery, as housing God's incomprehensible otherness. But can we dare to believe that the mystery hidden for ages and generations is actually being manifested *in us*? Is the believing community today, now divested of the triumphal trappings of the past, this people of God sojourning through history and bearing the poverty of its own sinfulness, is this church still a place where men and women experience the merciful closeness of God?

I confess to being a natively optimistic person. As I look at some of the recent developments in the church, I see grounds for disappointment and some discouragement, for there are those in the church who would like to reverse the direction and forces set in motion by Vatican II. There are many who have dropped out of the church, especially younger people, who have been disillusioned with things like poorly celebrated liturgies and frightfully uninspired preaching, the failure to include women fully in church life, or what appears to be a clerical preoccupation with sexual morality. They may have been swamped by the unbelief of our age and the church has not equipped them with a spirituality sturdy enough to weather the lure of economic success and a miserably dull picture of personal fulfillment.

Yet beyond this I see other more positive signs which indicate that the church has entered a brand new epoch. The growing spiritual and theological sensitivity on the part of Catholic thinkers and missionaries toward the other world religions, the vibrancy of the Latin American church and its theology, and the slow but steady inclusion of the experience and concerns of women in the life of the church and in theological reflection—these are wonderfully welcome developments. Many Catholics have made a breakthrough into a splendidly rich consciousness of being Christian and being church. The faith and the church have become freshly their own. They have realized, to a degree that counts, the historical relativity of human institutions (especially religious ones, like ecclesiastical structures, laws and practices) without yielding to disrespect or disregard for their Catholic Christian tradition. They have accepted the weaknesses and sinfulness of the church without necessarily giving up on institutional religion, for they have realized that they too, as the people of God, are the church. They are impatient for certain changes—for a more truly democratic church, for a more authentically evangelical church, for a church which can lead them into a richer experience of God. They are impatient but not reckless. Such developments should serve as important confirmations of the Spirit's abiding presence in the church and the world.

One of the major decrees of the Second Vatican Council is devoted to the nature of revelation. The Council emphasized what has come to be the major contemporary approach to the theology of revelation. It interpreted revelation in personal rather than conceptual terms as the process of God's self-communication, citing the Letter to the Ephesians: "In his goodness and wisdom, God chose to reveal himself and to make known to us the hidden purpose of his will." I would add a slight twist to this formulation. God is *still being revealed*, since from our standpoint men and women are continually being introduced to the holy mystery of God. God's self-communication continues to take place in a number of ways: in the desires of the human heart, in the questioning and wondering of the human mind, in our thirst for true freedom, in the life, death, and resurrection of Jesus, in the experience of having been loved and forgiven, in the conviction that we have been personally called to know and follow Jesus, in countless circumstances of daily life, and in the deep-down sense that we are meant to carry the divine presence within us. Once revelation is defined as the ongoing process of God's meeting us, the way is paved for looking at revelation in terms of what happens to men and women as they come closer to the mystery of God. And that is what this book is about.

The opening chapter presents an inverse approach to revelation. Instead of viewing revelation as God's coming out of hiddenness toward us (or as God's manifesting truths to us which our minds, unaided, could never have arrived at), I suggest that revelation might more fittingly be seen as our coming out of hiding into the light created by the holy mystery of God.

Chapter Two examines the notion of revelation by looking at

the mind's way of believing. Revelation is not the communication of something which is essentially foreign or unintelligible to us; otherwise, our minds would rebel against Jesus' call to faith. The mind is already in a situation of faith and of grace. The human mind is already comprehended by the holy mystery of God. And what is that situation like? What are the spiritual, human conditions under which we spend our lives? Here I have portrayed three experiential situations, three modes in which the process of our coming out of hiding takes place. There is journeying, there is aggrieved feeling over injustice and sin in the world, and there is being in love. One of these modes or situations (and there may be others) will be the "there" in which a Christian lives.

The third chapter is about the religious experience of Jesus' disciples. If revelation occurs anywhere, it happens in the context of people's experience. What are some of the features of the religious experience of the disciples? That is an important question since our experience, insofar as it is rooted in the gospel, is patterned after theirs. When the disciples experienced Jesus, the one who stood so freely in the Father's presence that he had nothing to hide, they touched and loved the perfect reflection of the Father's glory, a glory which they had been called to share.

The fourth chapter continues to develop the idea that the mystery of God shows itself within ordinary human experience. It seems to me that many of us simply do not believe that the kingdom of God has been unfolding in the midst of our lives. The very ordinariness of things keeps us from taking our own life situations seriously as places where we are becoming present to God. That's a pity. Unlike the movies, in daily life there is no musical score to draw attention to crucial moments, no easy resolutions, no sudden displays of divine transcendence, no editing for smoothness, no special effects to dramatize illusions so as to make them appear real. Either we learn to see that revelation unfolds in the lives of ordinary men and women like ourselves, or the notion of revelation will remain one more religiously unappetizing idea.

The last chapter addresses the connection between revelation and the will of God. It grows out of my own experience of religious life, but the point of the chapter has a wider Christian application.

To live in the presence of God, to come trustingly out of the hiding into which sin would pull us, is to experience ourselves and our lives with the freedom of the children of God. But the will of God has been for many Christians an imprisoning idea, not a liberating one. Some people speak too casually about something happening because it is "the will of God." They maintain a little too submissively that whatever happens ought to be humbly accepted. Occasionally we are instructed to obey those who have authority over us because what they tell us to do (or to think) is what God wills for us. It may sound as if those who hold positions of religious authority are revealing the will of God. If belief in the will of God is to be a freeing exercise of faith, then such conceptions must be pruned of their mythological and authoritarian overtones. And that is the point behind Chapter Five.

It is my hope that the contents of the book will resonate with the reader's own experience. I consider this to be a book about spirituality—the spirituality of revelation, to be precise. Although some ideas are developed in language which may sound formal, the concerns are always practical.

College of the Holy Cross
Worcester, Massachusetts
Feast of the Epiphany, 1987

CHAPTER 1

Adam in Hiding

> If you only understood how much repose is found in
> the way of wisdom, how much grace and how much
> sweetness! Don't go into hiding, don't be neglectful,
> but take up this journey and do not be afraid of the
> loneliness of the desert. . . . It is better for the one
> who is seeking the perfect life to die along the way
> than never to have started on the search for perfection.
>
> —Origen, *Homily on Joshua*[1]

Things are not always the way they seem, and a good
example of this is the idea of revelation. Revelation is not
exactly a matter of God's coming out of concealment toward
human beings. Rather, revelation describes our coming out of
hiding into the presence of God. But people do not generally think
of this when they hear the word *revelation*.

To *reveal* means "to unveil" or "to uncover"; it means emerging
from darkness and shadows into the light. Understood theologically, revelation has usually meant that God is hidden from us,
either because the divine mystery is so incomprehensible that our
finite minds could never grasp it, or because the human mind,
weakened by sin, has been deprived of its natural closeness to God,
and that this God has broken through our finitude, our ignorance,
and our sinfulness. In doing so, God draws us into the divine
mystery. This view of revelation implicitly advances at least three
important claims: It suggests, first, that the mystery of God is love;
second, that this love desires to draw us into union with itself; and
third, that if we are willing to allow God to come close to us, then
we shall be changed in the process to become more like God.

God, of course, does not dwell in shadows, and God has
nothing to hide. This fact makes it possible for us to develop yet
another perspective on revelation. The light of God's glory, the
mystery of God's love, might indeed so overwhelm our minds and

15

hearts as to cover them with a kind of darkness. But as the Psalmist says: "If I say, 'Surely the darkness will hide me and the light
become night around me,' even the darkness will not be dark to
you; the night will shine like the day, for darkness is as light to
you" (Ps 139:11-12). Our minds, so distracted by many things, so
unschooled in the proper manner of thinking toward God, have to
struggle to achieve clarity and wisdom. Yet the light which the
mind seeks, the light which somehow guides the mind in all its
efforts at genuine comprehension of what it means to be human, is
nothing less than the divine mystery itself. "Light from light, true
God from true God": The mystery of Christ is the mind's hidden
but real love. Coming to learn about this secret love which each of
us carries inside also belongs to the process of revelation.

The story which provides our clue as we look for deeper insight
into the meaning of revelation is told in the Book of Genesis:

> Then the man and his wife heard the sound of the
> LORD God as he was walking in the garden in the cool
> of the day, and they hid from the LORD God among the
> trees of the garden. But the LORD God called to the
> man, "Where are you?"
>
> He answered, "I heard you in the garden, and I was
> afraid because I was naked; so I hid."
>
> And he said, "Who told you that you were naked?"
> (Gn 3:8-11)

Notice that the man and the woman are the ones in hiding.
Crouched among the trees they want to avoid God's seeing them
and talking with them. God is the one who calls, "Where are
you?" What a telling question! Here God is asking Adam *where he
is*, and the where, it seems to me, is not simply a place, some dark
spot in the garden. God is asking about Adam's state: "What has
happened to you? What is this unnatural condition of being afraid
of me into which you have fallen?" Adam is closing his ears to the
voice of the one who made him, the one who knows him thoroughly, the one whose breath brought movement to his limbs.
Adam hides from the one who gave him life. Few questions unearth
so vividly the sadness and twisted vision behind human alienation.

If only Adam had remembered the truth:

> "Where can I go from your Spirit?
> Where can I flee from your presence? . . .
> My frame was not hidden from you
> when I was made in the secret place.
> When I was woven together in the depths of the earth,
> your eyes saw my unformed body" (Ps 139:7,15-16).

Adam is afraid of God—that says it all. Some terrible disorder has inserted itself into creation if men and women feel they have to conceal themselves in order to escape the gaze of the Lord.

What is intriguing, however, is God's question to Adam: "Who told you that you were naked?" The question seems to imply that being naked is the man's natural state. Being uncovered and totally open to God's view is the state God intended for us; it is the basic condition of our creaturehood. What reason is there to hide from God? And even if we had a reason, where on earth could we flee to avoid the divine presence? What dark place would remain dark to God's eyes? What is there about us that God does not know? No thought, no matter how secret or unformed, no desire, no fleeting fancy, no word or action whatsoever could escape God's hearing. Perhaps this strange need to hide lies at the root of most human sin. Why would we lie, except to keep someone from knowing what we have said, thought or done? How much of our arrogance, our stubbornness, or our greed "covers up" our inner poverty and loneliness?

Why do we think we must try to hide our real condition from God, or from one another, or even from our own selves? People deceive each other; they attempt to deceive God; they may succeed in deceiving themselves. But why do we hide? The anger toward others which frequently disguises some past hurt, the stubborn pride which often cloaks self-doubt, the materialism which masks inner emptiness, the excuses we invent for not praying, the way we rationalize why the words of a gospel passage do not apply to us—these are the signs that something has gone desperately wrong. "Who told you that you were naked?" In other words, What has led you to believe that your protection consists in running away from God's view? The whole mad story of alienation and sin begins with the effort to escape the presence of God. Flight, of course, is impossible, because God refuses to surrender Adam and Eve to the dominion of fear. They should not be afraid; they should not be in hiding. So the Lord God seeks out the creature, and the story of salvation is nothing less than the divine effort to uncover the creature, to unclothe it of all the pretense and deceit with which, in its fear, it has dressed itself in order to lie concealed from the eyes of God.

Thus, we might conclude, fear has disordered creation. Because of fear men and women have sought to hide, and the Lord God will not permit fear to imprison Adam and his descendants. Perhaps that explains why Paul wrote: "For you did not receive a spirit that makes you a slave again to fear, but you received the Spirit of sonship. And by him we cry, 'Abba, Father' " (Rom 8:15). Realizing Paul's fondness for the parallel between Christ and Adam, one is tempted to ask whether Paul was here envisioning Adam in fear hiding from the voice of God. To know God as Jesus knew God is to stand in the divine presence and to experience the freedom of the children of God. God, for Jesus, was not someone from whom we have to hide. For Jesus, God is the one who could be trusted absolutely, and this trust enabled Jesus to be fully human and free.

What, therefore, is revelation? Revelation means God's uncovering Adam so that he can experience God's love in his innermost self. Adam no longer has to steal into the shadows. Rather, Adam is drawn out of hiding into the presence of God. Adam does so because God refuses to leave him alone. The story of revelation is essentially the story of our coming to learn, to accept and to prize who we really are: daughters and sons of God. It is our nature to be, as Jesus was, completely uncovered to the eyes of God; to reject this would be to reject the possibility for any genuine and lasting joy.

There are more technically theological definitions of revelation available. Writers have elaborated on one or several aspects of revelation—what it is, how it occurs, how it is passed along from one generation to the next, the relation between revelation and scripture, or between revelation and doctrine, and so forth.[2] In recent years, theologians have been inquiring about whether divine revelation has been given to the human race only through the Judaeo-Christian tradition, or whether the divine mystery has also revealed itself to people who belong to other world faiths.[3] Some religious thinkers have distinguished *special* revelation from *general* revelation in order to safeguard the uniqueness of Christian faith. Others have regarded divine revelation more holistically. Revelation, they would urge, has been given to the entire world in a variety of more or less adequate ways. Yet basic to nearly every view of revelation is the belief that God has drawn mercifully close to human beings, that God has "spoken" to the world and made known the divine saving will for us. And equally central to many views of revelation is the conviction that the flesh and blood symbol which in an unsurpassable way communicates the great truth about God's coming close to us is Jesus Christ, the divine word made flesh.

The view I want to sketch in this chapter, however, leans on the way we *experience* the process of revelation. For here revelation does not so much consist of God's making Jesus known to us, or Jesus' making God known to us, but rather of God's making us known to ourselves by leading us into ever more familiar companionship with Jesus. Therefore, to develop the point that revelation consists in God's drawing Adam out of hiding, let us ask what truth God is so urgently trying to persuade Adam to believe in. For Paul that truth appears to have been the doctrine of justification.

Suppose someone came up to us, spotted a cheap necklace or ring we were wearing, and announced that he would give us a thousand dollars for it. We would probably protest that the piece of jewelry was not worth such a price. Yet imagine that the stranger then went on to offer a hundred thousand dollars, or even a million. We would look at him with astonishment, probably conclude he was crazy, and very likely insist that the item was not worth such a huge sum. But what does the concept of worth tell us? Isn't the worth of a thing determined by what people are willing to pay for it?

Now, suppose God wanted to teach us how much we are truly

worth. What price might God offer? Our real worth, after all, can only be determined by God, and in God's sight we are priceless. God is the buyer; it is God who redeems us. Thus, God decrees the price; God dictates our value. Our true worth, therefore, has nothing to do either with our sinfulness or our virtue, with our mistakes or our obedience. God unilaterally pronounces what our genuine value is: "But God demonstrates his own love for us in this: While we were still sinners, Christ died for us" (Rom 5:8). Our worth can only be measured in terms of the life of God's own Son. In drawing us to believe this profound truth about ourselves, God is justifying us; as we accept this truth with the obedient trust which characterized the life of Jesus, we are made righteous. After all, something may be priceless, but to the untrained eye it might appear worthless. So too in our case. We are invaluable in God's sight, but until we realize that fact, we terribly underestimate who and what we are. We do not lead our lives with that sense of wonder and freedom, that sense of personal honor and responsibility which comes from knowing that we are indeed God's children, that the Spirit of God has been poured into our hearts, and that we matter so dearly to God that only the crucified Jesus could tell us to what lengths God would go in teaching us of that love. Now, if this is how God proves the meaning of divine justice—a justice so extraordinarily rich that it must at the same time be called mercy and grace—what could we possibly be afraid of? Hence Paul writes:

> What, then, shall we say in response to this? If God is for us, who can be against us? He who did not spare his own Son, but gave him up for us all—how will he not also, along with him, graciously give us all things? Who will bring any charge against those whom God has chosen? It is God who justifies. Who is he that condemns? Christ Jesus, who died—more than that, who was raised to life—is at the right hand of God and is also interceding for us. Who shall separate us from the love of Christ? Shall trouble or hardship or persecution or famine or nakedness or danger or sword? . . . No, in all things we are more than conquerors through him who

loved us. For I am convinced that neither death nor life, neither angels nor demons, neither the present nor the future, nor any powers, neither height nor depth, nor anything else in all creation, will be able to separate us from the love of God that is in Christ Jesus our Lord (Rom 8:31-35,37-39).

In Romans 5:10 Paul speaks about our being God's enemies: "For if, when we were God's enemies, we were reconciled to him through the death of his Son, how much more, having been reconciled, shall we be saved through his life!" But, strictly speaking, God has no enemies. I suggest that we rethink this verse so that the sense reads "when we (mistakenly) believed that God was our enemy." If we could listen in on Paul's thinking, perhaps we would hear him wondering about what happened in Eden such that, as a result, human beings believed that God had become hostile to them. How could we ever think that God was our enemy?

Furthermore, Paul would continue, what did Jesus do for us? Jesus reconciled us to the Father; or rather, God reconciled the world to himself in Christ. God would not permit hostility to be the determining note in the divine-human relationship. In order to show this, God became vulnerable to human sin, vulnerable to the disordering fear which, because it cannot avoid the divine gaze, seeks instead to blind it. In the crucified Jesus God uncovered the face of sin so that we could see what we have done to ourselves. God sees us through the cross of Jesus, and through the cross of Jesus we contemplate the face of God. In this double vision the fearful urge to flee the divine presence is finally overcome. The story of our creation finishes on Calvary, not in Eden: "If anyone is in Christ, he is a new creation; the old has gone, the new has come! All this is from God, who reconciled us to himself through Christ" (2 Cor 5:17-18). It is the light of the cross which finally chases Adam out of hiding. The twisted figure of the dying Jesus captures the long bloody history of human beings trying to pretend that God has been their enemy: "God made him who had no sin to be sin for us, so that in him we might become the righteousness

of God" (2 Cor 5:21). With the crucified Jesus, the pretense, the
running away, is over at last.

There may be good reason for us to be afraid of coming out of
hiding. The story of Jesus shows us that when a human being, freed
by the love of God to be fully human and trusting, does live in the
light and openness of faith, he or she might well be drawn into the
mystery of the cross, the suffering which human beings inflict on
one another when they run from the love which could set them
free. Jesus naked on the cross, uncovered to God's view in the
obedience of his faith, awakens us to what can happen to those
who are not afraid to hear and respond to God's voice.

The Church as Situation in Which Revelation Occurs

Human community is the natural and normal context in which
the grace of Christ given to each one of us unfolds. By "the grace
of Christ" I mean that power at work in our mind and affections,
our desires and fantasies, our will and imagination, which creatively
fashions us into the likeness of Christ. The grace of Christ rightly
refers to other realities also—to the mercy and forgiveness of God
which Jesus has made available to us, to the experience of being
loved and accepted by the Father. But here I want to describe grace
from its dynamic side, for the grace of Christ is the holy mystery
unfolding in our midst; it uncovers us, and in doing so it forms
who we are and shapes what we shall become.

Now, from a religious point of view, not every gathering of men
and women is a community. People may live and work together;
they may eat and sleep together. But this does not guarantee that
they really live for one another, that they are mindful of each
other, or that they are helping each other to become fully human
and free. Given the fact that so many fail in their promises to
remain faithful to someone else, and that people often deceive,
take advantage of, or rashly judge friends, acquaintances and
strangers, we cannot presume that most human beings are actually
living a communal existence. That is why the church can, and
ought to, be a clearing in the world's wilderness. The Christian
community becomes the place where men and women can begin to

experience belonging to others, existing for others, being drawn personally and caringly into one another's life stories.

The reality which is church requires continual renewal. We have to work at being church and truly being people of God. Being church implies wanting to belong to one another. And in Christ we see what that belonging to others means. In Christ we find the way to ongoing renewal; we find the style of being human without which genuine community remains forever impossible. To be human, in Christ, means to live with and for others; it demands service, the readiness to forgive, and the willingness to let others help shoulder our burdens and share our hopes. These are things which we cannot accomplish without God's assistance. Likewise, we need other people—Christian friends—to teach us about being human and to help us escape from our fears and pretenses. The church, the Christian community, is that situation in which our coming out of hiding takes place. In living and building the reality which is Christian community, we enable one another to take off whatever masks our true selves and to be the free human beings which God intends for us to be.

An Illustration: Sacraments as Revelatory Moments

The idea of revelation we have been developing is that revelation is the process whereby God calls us out of hiding. One place where we observe the church's faith in action is Christian worship. Sacramental symbolism shapes our Christian consciousness. How could we express more completely our union with Christ, our commitment to follow him and his teaching, or our belief that the Spirit of Jesus inevitably leads us into communion with other men and women, than in sharing the one bread and the one cup? The chief elements of our faith—the creative love of God, the divine desire to reconcile the world in Christ, the need for trusting obedience on our part, the person and saving ministry of Jesus, the communion of saints and the community of believers called the church, the Spirit's active and continuing presence among us empowering us to believe and to hope, our expectation of the eventual fulfillment of all things in Christ—these beliefs Christians

hear, reflect on, and assent to again each time they join to pray the
Eucharist. There are other aspects of faith, to be sure, but liturgy is
an authoritative source of faith because Christians regularly find
the presence of God there.

Liturgy is also an aspect of the process of revelation. In liturgy
the church reminds us of what we believe as it proclaims the great
mystery of faith—that Jesus died, that he rose from the dead, and
that the final triumph of grace in this world belongs to those who
have learned to love God. But in liturgy we are also uncovered,
drawn out from the recesses of our isolation, our self-centering
behavior, our unhealthy tendencies to make our relationship with
God private, and our sinfulness. Liturgy draws us into community,
into the circle of faith, into the liberating air of repentance and
reconciliation. It uncovers us to the love of God which enables us
to live with our weakness without surrendering to discouragement.

Sacraments, then, are disclosures; they tell us various things
about ourselves. In particular they speak to us about who we are in
relationship to Christ, and they have their effect to the degree that
we permit our sacramental worship to pull us out of ourselves into
the freedom and truth which is Christ among us. One of the first
things generally explained about sacraments is that they are signs or
symbols. Through these symbols, provided we allow them to speak
to us and provided the church enacts them reverently and meaningfully, the healing, transforming power of the gospel reaches us.
Sacraments are flesh-and-blood, worldly, incarnational realities, and
the first sacrament is Jesus Christ. He is God's word-made-flesh, the
flesh-and-blood sign of the closeness and compassion of our unseen
God. For those who live in the company of Jesus, the reality of
God—what the New Testament refers to as the kingdom of God—
circumscribes their imagining and planning, their relating to
others, and every aspect of their experience. Men and women
encounter the holy mystery of God in countless ways through the
created world, through human relationships, through daily work
and the ordinary activities of life. They also meet God through
their bodiliness, through the workings of their minds and hearts,
and especially in their friendships. To say that the grace of God is

incarnational means simply that any reality in this world can be an instance of God's speaking to us.

Although we use the term *spirituality*, we must not be misled by the "spirit" part of the term. Christian spirituality is thoroughly rooted in this world; it is of the earth and everyday things just as much as the parables and examples Jesus employed in his teaching. Spirituality denotes what we are essentially: We are, in the phrase of the German Jesuit theologian Karl Rahner, "spirit-in-the-world." Not, mind you, spirits who happen to be living in the world, nor some combination of two contrasting elements like spirit and matter. We are enfleshed spirit, a single created reality. Spirit marks our deepest self, namely, that nerve or dimension of our being which keeps us authentically, humanly alive. Sacraments should be reminding us, even though we may categorize them as things which nourish our "spiritual" life, that we can never lay aside our human-ness. For Jesus was a human being, a person of flesh and blood, like us. In his person, as God's word to us, Jesus dissolved the barrier between the Temple (or the church) and the world, between the sanctuary (the realm of the sacred) and everyday life. That is why Jesus has been called the new Temple. The preaching of Jesus never suggested that he had his eyes on "super-natural," other-worldly realities. His metaphors and images about the kingdom of God were often taken from down-home scenes to which his listeners had no trouble relating. He spoke, not about philosophical or theologi-cal matters, but about wineskins, a mustard seed, wedding ban-quets, and so on. Indeed, the purpose for Jesus' speaking and teaching this way had to be his desire to help ordinary men and women get in touch with the mystery of God—the mystery of their life—which was unfolding each day in their midst. Jesus tried to move people away from concerns which distracted them from their true selves, from being really alive, from hearing the God who was calling them out of hiding.

We are creatures of flesh and blood. Therefore, this world is the only place where God can meet us. What feelings and thoughts come to me when I read about an earthquake in Mexico, about a volcano erupting and destroying a village in Colombia, about demonstrations against nuclear weapons, about protests against apartheid in South Africa, about hunger in the United States? What do my reactions or my desires tell me about myself? What about the hopes I entertain for my family, my efforts to escape loneliness, or my fears of rejection, of becoming dependent on others as my body ages and weakens, of losing my memory, of being unemployed? What do concerns like these tell me about myself? What about my anxiety that my life might not have been well spent, that I have wasted time, talents or opportunities? What do I hunger for more than anything else? Do I ever imagine myself facing Jesus, and if so, do I talk with him about the next life or about this one? Questions of this sort indicate the possible points of contact between us and God. They help us to open up our experience to the word of God. We shall never be able to enter into God's concerns unless we have first found God entering into ours. We approach the church's sacramental worship out of such questions, worries, fears, hopes and dreams. They represent the real situation of our life in this world, and we can legitimately expect that somehow the word of God will address us there, right in the thick of our very ordinary humanity. If God's word speaks to some aspect of our life or experience, then our living has indeed become blessed.

What, after all, is a blessing but a gesture of unveiling? Whenever the church blesses, it uncovers to the eye of faith that original blessing which God conferred upon creation when, surveying and approving the divine handiwork, God saw that everything was good. Through its practice of blessing created things, and especially through its sacramental worship, the church builds up our faith vision so that we can perceive ever more sharply the original blessing God pronounced over creation. Each sacrament recovers the original goodness of some created reality. It enables us to appreciate and thank God for the inherent goodness of something close to us whose value we may have come to take for granted: family life, community, friendship, food, meal-taking, our desire for God. The liturgy of each sacrament draws our attention to the conditions which must be met if that original blessing is to appear:

commitment, trust, reconciliation and forgiveness, service, obedience to God, prayerful recollection, gratitude, reverence for the
earth.

Baptism, for instance, uncovers the fact that we are sons and
daughters of God. Baptism does not make us children of God for
the first time; we are so by virtue of the fact that God has created
us, and whatever God does is good and blessed. But baptism is the
occasion when the church helps us to understand and acknowledge
who and what we are, that we have come from God, that we are
loved by God, and that our ultimate destiny transcends our existence on this earth. All this is gift, of course, original gift. The
baptismal blessing unveils it. Yet baptism also inaugurates something new. Through the sacramental rite the Spirit creates a
relationship between the individual and Christ, a relationship
which marks and seals the person's life with the mystery of Jesus'
dying and rising. For those whose faith lets them perceive it, this
relationship uncovers the profoundest human possibility; namely,
that men and women can become like Christ, the one with whom
God was so well pleased.

Baptism and the sealing with the Spirit (I take *confirmation* to
be the liturgical completion of baptism) also initiate a relationship
between the individual and the Christian community. The church
sees this relationship as permanent and unbreakable because it
reflects and uncovers God's permanent, irreversible love for us. But
Christian community itself is a new, distinct human possibility
which will exist only if men and women freely decide to follow
Jesus together. Christian community is different from other human
gatherings because it is comprised of people who know they are
sinners, who believe they are loved, and thus who have no reason
to be afraid. The church—the believing community—always stands
in need of conversion and renewal. The church does not exist apart
from its members' willingness to forgive and accept one another, to
live according to the teaching and example of Jesus, and to recall
faithfully and regularly the meaning of his death and resurrection.
In other words, baptism uncovers the conditions for true and

lasting community. Baptism tells us that there can be no real communion apart from the Spirit of God. Genuine community is always God's gift; it should never be taken for granted.

Whatever baptism uncovers, *Eucharist* uncovers all the more. The Eucharist is the church's continuing celebration of baptismal grace. Eucharist recovers the fact that we are made for communion, that we have a basic human desire to be one with others, and that God is the source of this lifegiving desire. The conditions for community are again laid bare: a common acknowledgement of sinfulness and dependence upon God, the forgiving and accepting of others as our brothers and sisters, the readiness to take food together as a sign of our shared need for bread, and the remembering that we belong to one another because we belong to Christ. Eucharist uncovers the reality of our being church, for at the eucharistic assembly the community calls the individual out of hiding, out of isolation, out of any refusal to admit that he or she belongs to Christ and to his brothers and sisters, away from fear. The community lures the individual away from the lonely security of private faith into that welcome freedom which arises from being known, forgiven and loved by someone else.

Reconciliation too is a continuing celebration of baptismal grace. The forgiveness which God extends to us at baptism does not merely extend to past sins (in the case of infants, of course, there are none). As we recite it in the creed, baptism for the forgiveness of sins anticipates that God will always be there for us, always ahead of us with the same mercy and grace with which we are being daily created. On the basis of our baptism we have the courage to trust that despite our unfaithfulness God will not abandon us or cease caring.

The importance of this belief can take years to sink in. We may reach a stage in our lives when we simply do not care about God, about religion, or about right and wrong. If we could actually do so, we might even tell God to leave us alone, that we know exactly what we are doing, and that we want no more part with Christ or his church. After all, since we have no guarantee that we shall not one day feel estranged and divorced from people who are now very close to us, why should it be surprising if we wind up feeling this way toward God? But whereas we could easily succeed in driving away our family and friends, God does not take us at our word. And this is our salvation, because in moods of desperation and defiance, even in the coolness of separation, we very likely still do not know what we truly want, or what we ultimately care about, or what finally could bring us peace. Even if a mother abandons her child—presumably not out of a loss of maternal affection but out of exasperation with a child who has turned away from her love—God says, "I will not forget you." The sacrament of reconciliation uncovers this truth for the believing community in its moments or seasons of erring and estrangement. Reconciliation exposes human sinfulness and uncovers the heart's yearning for healing, for love and for acceptance.

Of all the sacraments, reconciliation has probably had the most checkered history. Among the early Christian communities it was celebrated rarely. In fact, for a while frequent imparting of absolution was not only discouraged but forbidden. The Eucharist remained the normal liturgical place for receiving forgiveness of sin. In time confession and communion became routine Catholic practice. Today sacramental confession is celebrated with much less frequency than, say, 25 years ago, and there are a variety of reasons for this which I shall not develop here. One thing can be said, however. The church needs to develop and encourage the communal form for celebrating this sacrament. We have come very far as a believing community in realizing the implications of the fact that the Spirit of God characteristically draws people together. People today are not sinning less than before (although a number of the failings they formerly identified as sinful were improperly labeled), but they are noticing that all sin, whether public or solitary, affects the life of the community. The word of forgiveness will feel incomplete to many of us unless those who have been particularly affected by our sin are in some way visibly involved when the church extends to us the peace of Christ.

Marriage uncovers human friendship at its most personal level, for the one thing which God declared not good was that Adam should be alone. This sacramental friendship draws people into community and solidarity so strongly that, for most Christians, the marriage relationship becomes the clear, lighted space where they experience God and become like Christ. The church regards the love between husband and wife to be permanent and unbreakable because God meant it to reflect the permanence of God's own love for the world. The trusting commitment to another person for life creates the situation in which the two of them together become fully human and free. Marriage is not only a special form of human community, it is also the place in which most Christians will look for and discover God. Marriage is the foundation for family life and the first experience most of us have of being church.

The love of God and the love of neighbor are not two loves but one. My love for God and my love for my friend are one. A husband's love for his wife and the wife's love for her husband, together with the love each has for God, are one love. Marriage unveils the mystery of human love, and so it also illumines the mystery of our loving and being loved by God. Why? Because love is one, even if there are many whom I love and even if there are many who draw love out of me.

To love God is the supreme exercise of human freedom. It is to turn toward the One who is constantly creating us and to welcome the grace which daily fashions and refashions the human heart. There is a transforming power in love; we are changed to the degree that we love. We become newly-made the more we allow love to claim our soul, our liberty, our mind, our strength.

Marriage is the uncovering of the mystery of human love, for the love of God and our love for the friend whom we marry is a single love. It might not appear that way, since religious love is not normally associated with passion, with romance and with the most intimate of personal union. Yet human love is necessarily sacramental. All loving derives from the One who first loves the human world. Thus, all human loving sacramentalizes—symbolizes and makes present—that first and original love. Christian marriage uncovers this truth.

Every human community depends upon certain individuals to oversee its functioning, its well-being, and its survival. So too in the church. The *sacrament of orders* uncovers this essential aspect of our being human together. For the church, however, this involves more than the need for men and women to exercise various ministries, since many of the church's ministries do not presuppose sacramental ordination, only baptism. In orders a Christian makes a lifelong commitment to the Christ who dwells among his brothers and sisters, taking special care for the community's liturgical life and for its constant attentiveness to the scriptural word. The ordained minister is the community's personal sign of its dependence upon the great sacramental symbols which uncover its life. The ordained minister personalizes the community's need to live under the word of God, to hear that word proclaimed and interpreted. The priest is the community's public witness—the church's public voice—of its daily need for forgiveness and reconciliation. Accepting the church's charge daily to remember his brothers and sisters before the Lord, the priest testifies to the fact that such concern for the life of the community deserves the total dedication of one's life. Ordained ministry helps to uncover the abiding presence of Christ in the church and Christ's promise to be with his disciples until the end of time.

Other Christians also pray for the church. Others can be agents of reconciliation and the Lord's peace. Some even celebrate the sacraments, since any Christian can, if necessary, baptize, and it is the married couple, not the priest, who sacramentalize their love. But Christ's fidelity to the church, as the one who strengthens the faith of his disciples through word and sacrament, needs to be uncovered by public witness and personalized.

The sacrament of orders also discloses a further aspect of human sinfulness. Communities can fail. Such failure may occur because so few are willing to spend themselves selflessly for the sake of building community. The hireling works only for pay; the shepherd does not. Communities can collapse because so few call them to renewal, or labor to heal divisions, or risk rejection in order to finger waywardness and injustice. A community can fail because its leaders do not provide credible example of the human values needed to sustain the community's life. The ordained minister is the way by which the people of God reminds itself that without a public, personal, lifelong sign, important dimensions of the mystery of God will not be uncovered.

The *anointing of the sick* likewise is an occasion in which a feature of our basic human condition is uncovered. In this case the experience is that of sickness, aging and death. A person can, of course, try to run away from these things, but they are an inevitable part of the human situation and our happiness will never lie in fleeing what we cannot change. There is no pretending that we are not mortal. There is no hiding from the common lot of humanity.

But diminishment need not appear to us as evil. We do not have to be alienated from this aspect of our humanness. Sickness, aging and the slow disintegration which leads to death can reveal a blessing. No one will discern this blessing without faith. The believing Christian, for all of his or her belief in eternal life, will not be overly hasty in attempting to leave this one. Yet illness and dying do offer us an opportunity to say yes, profoundly and maybe quite painfully, to the mysterious providence which makes by unmaking, which finishes our creation by permitting us to feel the steady unweaving of what it has taken a lifetime to accomplish. The anointing of the sick sacramentalizes the Lord's concern that, even as we sense our energies being withdrawn, we should not think that God has begun to desert us or that God no longer has any interest in us because we are physically, and perhaps mentally, unready for divine service. Rather, the same love which called us into existence remains our gift, and will remain so forever. But we have to accept this in an almost blind faith for we have nothing left to bargain with, little left to offer God in terms of what we might actually do for Jesus and our neighbor. We have no place to hide from the uncertainty which lies ahead of us.

Death is frightening. At the very least it leaves us wondering about paths not chosen, about infidelity, about days and weeks when we had been oblivious to the important and precious events and people which God had given us.

Yet there is a blessing here too, and it has to do with power being made perfect in weakness. If the process during which we are called upon to surrender our pretenses, the headiness of our self-determining behavior, even to relinquish—regretfully—a world and people whom we have greatly loved, if this process does become our final and most personal expression of faith that even here God is with us, then we shall have found the blessing in the experience. Death may be painful, especially the more aware we are of its advent, but it is not necessarily evil. It becomes evil the more we refuse it.[4]

If, during life, we have given expression to our faith through the daily activities wherein we die a little to ourselves, wherein we suffer disappointment patiently and without overly complaining, wherein we have stayed faithful to Jesus even when such fidelity exacted its toll, then our dying will not appear evil. Having lived with Christ, we shall already have accepted our dying. We shall have already begun to die with him. On the other hand, if we lived with compromise, if we did not take up the cross and follow Jesus each day, if we held onto our bitterness, our selfishness and our pride, if we habitually put ourselves before others, if we have been guilty of self-deception as to how genuinely interested we were in being companions of Jesus, if we avoided occasions to show generosity and courage, then death will appear to be our enemy. Dying is our last opportunity to decide that, finally, human existence comes from God and that our chief business in life is to learn how to love the holy mystery of God. In one way or another, all this is being said to us in the church's sacramental anointing.

The sacraments also reveal what we are hiding from. Through them the church signals where we might be tempted to escape the challenges of being human: the flight from commitment, for it is seldom easy to stand by our word and to own our actions; the flight from being known, for opening ourselves to others generally entails the exposure of those myths we entertain about our virtue and personal accomplishments; the flight from forgiving others, for we may be shamed into having to ask for forgiveness in return, or we may prefer to savor the taste of resentment and hurt feelings; the flight from intimacy, for so much inside of us craves privacy and independence; the flight from sharing and service; the flight from those things that spell diminishment and suffering, for we fear death and we do not really trust that the mystery of Jesus' death must encompass our dying too. We flee these things because we are afraid.

At root, I think, we are running away from intimacy with God as Adam did. It is one thing to want God to be available in our needs, in our hour of struggle, in our rejection and hurt; to want to be consoled with a sense of divine beauty and goodness. But it is quite another thing to be available to God, to be prepared to be drawn into God's concerns, and to pay attention to the divine lament over the world's grief, its poverty and its self-centering greed; to be pulled into an awareness of how much the world pleads with us for help in its hunger and thirst for justice. Intimacy is not difficult when we share our joys, but it becomes a burden when we need to share our sinfulness. It is often easier to eat our food and withdraw inwardly from the openness and sharing which meal-taking symbolizes than to face the challenge of learning to like and to listen to one another. The Eucharist should chase this demon out of hiding and speak to us firmly about why Jesus chose to do so much of his Father's work around the table, and why so many gospel texts allude to banquets, feasts, cups of wine and breaking bread. For Jesus it appears that meal-taking was the privileged expression of human intimacy and therefore the only carry-over from the present life into the kingdom. No marriages, no baptisms, no confirmations, no confessions there. But Jesus does envision sitting at God's table with his sisters and brothers.

In revelation God takes the first step toward us. That step consists in our being invited to come out of hiding into the light of God's presence. Revelation is the mystery of our being uncovered. It is the mystery of our consenting to become luminous and transparent to the eye of God. The one "who loves God is known by God," Paul wrote (1 Cor 8:3), and again, "Now that you know God—or rather are known by God . . ." (Gal 4:9). Even after Christ, or perhaps precisely because of Christ, God remains un-speakably more than our minds can understand or our hearts can embrace. But that we should experience ourselves as men and women who have been known, whose inner being has been penetrated by the healing, creative gaze of the One whom Jesus called Abba, whose most secret words never escape the Father's notice, this belongs to the mystery of our being revealed. And the church? The church is the site of those sacramental celebrations which disclose the rich depths of full human living. The church should be that place where we learn to let God see us, hear us and make us free. It should be the place where we meet the love that casts out fear.

FOOTNOTES

1. Hans Urs von Balthasar, *Origen: Spirit and Fire*, trans. Robert J. Daly (Washington, D.C.: Catholic University of America Press, 1984), p. 66.

2. For a full discussion of various approaches to the theology of revelation, see Avery Dulles, *Models of Revelation* (New York: Doubleday & Co., 1983).

3. See Paul Knitter, *No Other Name?* (Maryknoll, NY: Orbis Books, 1985).

    Two seminal essays by Karl Rahner are still very much worth reading: "History of the World and Salvation-History" and "Christianity and the Non-Christian Religions." These appear in volume five of his *Theological Investigations* (Baltimore: Helicon Press, 1966).

    See also Walter Kasper, *The God of Jesus Christ* (New York: Crossroad Publishing Co., 1984), pp. 116-130.

4. On the difference between Jesus' death and our death, see Sebastian Moore, *The Crucified Jesus Is No Stranger* (New York: Seabury Press, 1977), pp. 56-68.

CHAPTER 2

Thinking About God and Believing: Letting God Reveal the Mind to Itself

Another benefit that comes from the revelation to men of truths that exceed the reason is the curbing of presumption, which is the mother of error. For there are some who have such a presumptuous opinion of their own ability that they deem themselves able to measure the nature of everything; I mean to say that, in their estimation, everything is true that seems to them so, and everything is false that does not. So that the human mind, therefore, might be freed from this presumption and come to a humble inquiry after truth, it was necessary that some things should be proposed to man by God that would completely surpass his intellect.

Now, the knowledge of the principles that are known to us naturally has been implanted in us by God; for God is the Author of our nature. These principles, therefore, are also contained by the divine Wisdom. Hence, whatever is opposed to them is opposed to the divine Wisdom, and, therefore, cannot come from God. That which we hold by faith as divinely revealed, therefore, cannot be contrary to our natural knowledge.
                                        —St. Thomas Aquinas[1]

One difficulty that we need to be alert to as we try to grow religiously is our craving for the miraculous. Many devout people believe that God has intervened in history in an extraordinary way through the Judaeo-Christian tradition. But since they have not personally witnessed divine interventions such as they read about in the Bible, their faith remains unsteady. They are ever on the lookout for proof that God is present in the world and

campaigning on the Christian side. Some people defend the literal
interpretation of the biblical stories of God's miraculous dealings
with the people of Israel because they want to find in those stories
concrete evidence for God's becoming dramatically involved in
human affairs. Once again, however, things are not always the way
they seem.

The Second Vatican Council distinguished between God's self-
revelation through words and through events. There are the utter-
ances which a prophet, for example, decisively spoke on God's
behalf because the word of the Lord had been given to him. And
there are the mighty deeds or displays of power by which people
were led to place their faith and trust in God. Devout people with
interventionist leanings will point to such instances and assert,
"Here, you see, God has certainly intervened in human history."

The Council, noting that the divine plan of revelation is
nothing less than our being invited into communion with God,
teaches:

> This plan of revelation is realized by deeds and words
> having an inner unity: the deeds wrought by God in the
> history of salvation manifest and confirm the teaching
> and realities signified by the words, while the words
> proclaim the deeds and clarify the mystery contained in
> them.[2]

We should notice, however, that deeds and actions need to be
interpreted. Otherwise they will simply leave people perplexed.
Even the miraculous healings which Jesus performed had to be
explained. After all, some people observed them and concluded
that Jesus was working through the power of the devil. So Jesus
(through the gospel writer) had to draw the connection between his
healings and the arrival of God's kingdom, or between the freeing
from physical handicap and the forgiveness of sins. To take another
example, the empty tomb of Jesus by itself left the disciples in the
dark. The empty tomb needed to be interpreted by an angel so that
the disciples could comprehend its connection with the Easter
event.

Something similar applies to the "word of the Lord," as scripture describes the prophetic message. The words of a prophet must be verified as being from God. Some one or some group has the task of authenticating the true prophet and of discrediting the false one. The community—the tradition of faith—eventually saw the prophetic word confirmed. The prophet himself might have been convinced that he spoke the truth, but how could the people to whom he addressed his message be expected to acknowledge immediately the source of the prophet's spirit and conviction? The process of acknowledging that spirit would take a while. At the time the prophet spoke there may not have been any compelling sign to make people mend their ways. It was not so easy as it sounds, centuries later, to discern the voice of God in the prophet's message. Think of how the world has treated some of its modern-day prophets—its Oscar Romeros, its Dorothy Days, its Martin Luther Kings. Think of how slow we are to accept the words and example of those who challenge us in the name of the gospel. In short, our interventionist leanings would probably not have been assuaged by those who professed to speak in God's name. No matter how powerfully and charismatically the prophets spoke, people did not escape the responsibility of making their own decision for rejecting or accepting the prophetic message. And, as Jesus said, if people did not believe the mighty prophets of old, they would not have been convinced of God's word even if they beheld someone raised from the dead!

It seems to me that the miraculous element is not the central characteristic of God's revealing action. Men and women normally become aware of the divine dimension in their human experience only gradually. In spite of the amazing details in their stories, the actual coming to faith of men and women in the Bible was most likely accomplished in the ordinary, everyday ways in which we too come to faith. To be sure, there are moments in our lives when we will be particularly aroused to believe in God. Certain events, both personal and historical, can plant us in the holy mystery of God firmly and deeply. Moments of crisis or decision, unexpected turns of fortune, displays of nature's power or beauty, even the signs of our times—the proliferation of nuclear weapons, political crises around the globe, revolutionary struggles for justice and freedom, a church council, the plight of refugees fleeing torture and oppression, ecological disasters—may stretch our faith, force us to wrestle with God, or become the occasion for a profound insight into that holy mystery which holds all of nature and history, every human life, in its embrace. Moments such as these prompt us to question ourselves or our society and its values. They may enrage us, reminding us of the inhumanity of which people are capable. They may challenge us to develop lasting concern for the world, to feel the link between our personal sinfulness and the predicaments of nations. They may even help us to spot the patient mercy of God working its way into human living and societies, now healing and forgiving, now inspiring people to spend their lives in service of their brothers and sisters. From this point of view everything can be miraculous; everything is potentially a word or deed in which the Lord is being made known to us, or through which we learn more about the holy mystery which is spreading across our lives. Yet for the most part faith grows slowly, steadily, usually imperceptibly, in ways not unlike the growing of the kingdom of God. "Then Jesus asked, 'What is the kingdom of God like? What shall I compare it to? It is like a mustard seed, which a man took and planted in his garden. It grew, and became a tree, and the birds of the air perched in its branches' " (Lk 13:18-19).

Faith would be made less risky, perhaps, if God were to appear to us in startling and magical ways, leaving no doubt about the fact that a sacred mystery has been passing through our world. But is that what revelation is all about? If we read the biblical account of an extraordinary event like the Exodus, for example, we learn that the people whom Moses led out of Egypt were not so overwhelmed by the display of divine power that they listened to Moses and obeyed the law of the Lord unswervingly. They were no sooner delivered from bondage than they began to grumble and complain because they missed their cucumbers! Even the Easter stories do not leave us with the assurance that the disciples, having seen the risen Jesus, believed in him unhesitatingly. I think we can safely generalize that, taking scripture on its own terms, the disposition to believe is an indispensable condition of God's being revealed to us. No matter how supernatural and astonishing a story about God's meeting human beings may sound, the dramatic sign which the interventionist side of us craves never forced people into believing. Each of us has probably experienced something similar. Having felt intimately close to God one week, consoled and strengthened by the divine presence, the next week we can find ourselves unwilling to spend any time in prayer, perhaps even doubting God's presence, God's concern, or whether God exists after all.

In order to counter our interventionist leanings, we have to insist that God is already in the world (to the degree that God can be said to be "in" anything), and that if God were not already in the world, already somehow in the fabric of human living and experiencing, then there would be no way of bringing God in. Why? Because we do not stand on an independent platform looking simultaneously at God and the world. We have no way of telling whether the voice breaking in from the outside is the divine voice or that of a human pretender. No way, that is, unless God is so creating us that we are already attuned to hearing the divine word. But if we are already attuned, then God has a foothold in the human world from the start. God is part of us. That part is already speaking to us about the holy mystery which has brought us into existence, and that is what revelation is all about.

In the first chapter we looked at the meaning of revelation as an experience of being uncovered, and we took our clue from the creation story in the Book of Genesis. In this chapter I want to explore another aspect of the revelation experience. Revelation should not be regarded as God's moving into or intervening in the human world from outside and beyond it. That way of viewing things does not do justice to our experience. The mystery of God unfolds from inside this world, from within human experience and from within human history. If we lead our lives waiting for God to show up in some miraculous way, then we shall not only wind up disappointed and perhaps even disillusioned with the whole business of religion and faith, but we shall also probably overlook many signs of the abiding closeness of God. That would be a tragedy. What could be worse than blindly searching for someone who has been with us all along?

The first point I want to consider is the spiritual problem

which arises when reason is divorced from faith. The mind already exists within the mystery of God, and the difficulty is that this fact is often overlooked by people as they begin thinking about and looking for God. The attempt to know God by reasoning alone before venturing into prayer, at least for most people, is bound to fail. This leads into a brief, explanatory account of the mind's act of faith and then into a broader description of three faith-situations in which people of God might find themselves, three situations in which the process of revelation occurs. These situations affect our thinking about God and they condition the way in which our relationships with God develop. In the course of the chapter it should become clear that to discuss revelation is also to lay the groundwork for a spirituality of thinking about God, whether one thinks about God in a simple, spontaneous, unsystematic manner, or in a highly refined, technical, theological way. After all, if creation is a gift, so too are human thinking and reasoning. Just as every breath we draw as creatures presupposes the gift of creation, so too every effort to think—especially to think about God— presupposes that goodness and love which fashioned human intelligence in the first place.

The Problem: What Keeps the Mind From Praying?

During my seminary formation, I was introduced to the practice of making an annual eight-day retreat. An experienced retreat director was invited to conduct the retreat, which usually involved presenting us with material for meditation. The director would follow the general outline of meditations in Ignatius Loyola's *Spiritual Exercises* and invariably the material for the first few meditations would be devoted to creation. The pattern was familiar. The creed we recited on Sundays also opened with a profession of faith in God as the creator of heaven and earth, and so did the catechism, as I remembered it from grammar school. The great systematic presentation of faith given by St. Thomas Aquinas in his *Summa Contra Gentiles* followed the order of God, creation, providence and salvation. The ordinary catechetical strategy, in short, was to proceed from the general notion of God as creator to the mysteries of Jesus' life, and to a specific notion of God as redeemer.

For me, this pattern—creation, redemption and sanctification—which the creed, the catechism, and many theology texts followed, suggested that the mind had to be eased from the mode of reason to the mode of faith, from so-called natural theology to theology proper, from what the mind can naturally know about God by the use of reason to what we know about God through revelation. In other words, it suggested that the best way to begin meditating and praying was to think about creation. If you thought correctly about creation, then you would have proven to yourself that there is a God behind it all to whom you could confidently address words of adoration, praise and thanksgiving. I must confess that I never got very far, because I never found my reasons or arguments for the existence of God to be sufficiently compelling, no matter how complex, intricate, beautiful, and awesome the works of creation appeared. My mind stumbled, my prayer was confused, and I developed a strong distaste for retreats.

But during one retreat about 10 years ago it occurred to me that the whole retreat enterprise, and in fact, the whole process of religious education, could begin with a different starting point. Just as we should not begin the study of theology by trying to demonstrate the existence of God, neither do we have to begin a retreat by enticing the mind into wondering and marveling over the fact of existence. The point came home to me with a vengeance when a student of mine, while trying to make a retreat, was simply unable to praise God for the gift of creation because he was not convinced of the reality of the "You" who is to be addressed in prayer. He struggled to reason his way into a relationship with God and wound up terribly frustrated by his mind's poor showing when it came to proving that God is really there. The underlying problem, as I saw it, was that he did not start from his experience, from the situation of his own life, but from an idea and a speculative question. He was attempting to settle a cosmological issue about the first cause of everything before his mind could relax and he could pray. Revelation, in other words, had been for him, as it had been for me, an intellectual or abstract affair. It was not an affair of the heart, or a matter of God's speaking within ordinary human experience.

However interesting cosmological issues might be in an astronomy course or a philosophy classroom, they are generally spiritual red herrings. The place to begin thinking about creation is our own experience of being created. We have to look at the whole situation in which the mind lives, not just the abstract or intellectual band of experience in isolation from the other aspects of our existence. In other words, creation is not finally an issue to be figured out by scientific analysis; creation is a dimension of revelation. Creation—not first causes or puzzles about the ultimate intelligibility of the cosmos—cannot be apprehended apart from faith. So too with revelation. The meaning of revelation—God's becoming known to us, our becoming known to God—arises from our experience of coming out of hiding into the fresh air of God's liberating presence.

From time to time I have noticed that students in my theology classes encounter a difficulty similar to the one I used to endure on retreats. They come to the course with faith, but when they have to start thinking critically about what they believe, they slip into assuming that they need to have their beliefs proven before they can continue as believers. If they don't find their beliefs explained to their satisfaction, they may not return to religious living for years. For the remainder of the course they seem unable to take the study of theology seriously. Somehow they let their minds get in the way of genuine thinking. They allow themselves to think apart from their experience, for the fact of the matter is that even while they think and question, the creative, revealing power of God works in their lives. But I am getting ahead of myself.

Creation itself is a grace, a grace in which we "live and move and have our being" (Acts 17:28), whether we realize it or not. To contemplate creation, therefore, is to reflect upon God's goodness and love. This is quite different from thinking about the philosophical arguments that might lend support to Christian belief. The psalmist writes:

> When I consider your heavens,
> the work of your fingers,
> the moon and the stars,
> which you have set in place,

what is man that you are mindful of him,
the son of man that you care for him? (Ps 8:3-4)

Here the contemplation of creation takes place in the context of prayer; the mind of the psalmist is already within a situation of faith. The reality of God does not have to be proven first.

Furthermore, the progression of ideas from God as creating and revealing to God as redeeming may represent the standard arrangement of Christian doctrines, but it does not necessarily reflect the arrangement of Christian experience. A person could begin a retreat, or the process of religious instruction, for instance, by meditating on the crucifixion or the Sermon on the Mount, and someone could compose a catechism or a theology text which would open with a discussion of the resurrection or the nature of Christian baptism. As a matter of fact, resurrection faith has to be presupposed in all genuine reflection upon and serious searching for God. Christian theology has to assume that the Spirit of the risen Jesus is always working in the world.

The relationship between reason and faith has been a recurrent issue in the history of Christian thought. That relation touches both spirituality and theology, and it underscores the fact that the life of prayer is inseparable from the life of the mind. Is it really possible to think about God without believing in God and praying to God? Although reason and faith are theoretically distinguishable, can they be separated in a person's life? It seems to me that they cannot.

The Believing Mind

Christian thinkers have frequently drawn attention to the distinction between reason and faith, or between reason and revelation. Often they wish to underline the fact that God's self-gift to human beings is absolutely gracious. "No one can come to me," Jesus says, "unless the Father who sent me draws him" (Jn 6:44). Because Christians believe that truth is one, that it proceeds from a single source, theologians have insisted that there should be some "fit" or congruence between the truth of revelation and the truth arrived at by human reason. According to this view reason and revelation are distinct but complementary.

The distinction between reason and faith, or between reason and revelation, can mean various things depending on how the terms are defined. Sometimes reason refers to the truths of reason, those things which the mind comes to know on its own. These are opposed to truths of faith, those things which the mind comes to know because God reveals them. According to this view, Christianity possesses a directory of revealed truths because God intervened in human history and provided them, primarily by inspiring the writings which comprise the Bible.

Today theologians are more likely to define truth, faith and revelation in personal terms. Truth is less a matter of correct propositions about natural or supernatural realities and more a matter of whatever transforms people in the direction of greater freedom, life and selfless love. Revelation is less a matter of divinely disclosed facts about supernatural things and more a matter of God's free, loving and personal closeness to us. Faith is less a matter of intellectual assent to religious beliefs and more a matter of the Christian's trusting surrender to the God who has become present to us in Jesus.

Even when truth, revelation and faith are taken in more conceptual and less personal terms, we must remember that human thinking is already a gift, that grace has been knit into the inner-most fibers of our minds and wills. Thus whatever the mind comes to know, even in a so-called natural way, about the things of this world, would be impossible without God's grace. The mind's ability and readiness to recognize the truth of religious belief rest upon the same grace. Without God's grace the mind could never arrive at truth, natural or otherwise. The absolute gratuity of God's love accounts for everything we are and everything that we might yet become. Perhaps, then, the mark of grace does not consist in the eminence of revealed truths over natural truths but in the transformation of heart and mind whereby a person really becomes a man or a woman of God.

Although nature and grace, the natural and supernatural, are to be distinguished, the reality of grace pervades the whole of creation. And this insight into the seamless fabric of nature and grace arises from Christian experience, for when Christians turn to prayer

the distinction between faith and reason grows less and less conse-
quential. The God of creation is also the God of Jesus. How would
the Christian discern a difference between the God who is present
in Jesus and the God who is present in creation? What practical
consequence would such a distinction serve? How significant, for
the Christian who prays, would the difference be between the God
of faith and the God of reason?

The same minds which study the world in order to clarify what
can be known about God through human reasoning also study
what is known about God because of the divine presence in Jesus
Christ. Whether thinking about so-called natural knowledge of
God or about God's revelation in Jesus, or about anything else for
that matter, the same mind is at work. Authentic human thinking,
it seems to me, always draws upon contemplation. Thus Hans Urs
von Balthasar writes: "It is only the man who has encountered the
living God in the particular form of revelation chosen by him who
can really find God in all things and, thus, who can truly and
constantly philosophize."[3]

At the end of his treatise *On the Incarnation*, St. Athanasius
remarked:

> He that would comprehend the mind of those who
> speak of God must needs begin by washing and cleans-
> ing his soul, by his manner of living, and approach the
> saints themselves by imitating their works; so that
> associated with them in the conduct of a common life,
> he may understand also what has been revealed to them
> by God.[4]

In short, a person cannot even begin to understand what those
who try to contemplate the mystery of God are talking about unless
his or her way of life has been set in order. Today we would say that
knowing the truth makes no sense apart from doing the truth, that
genuine knowledge is not achieved without asceticism, and that
there is no access to the God who is Father of Jesus Christ without
prayer and love for others.

Furthermore, the more we think about it, the more the distinction between faith and reason feels somewhat artificial. After all,

believers need to use their heads just as much as nonbelievers do. I have found that I cannot bracket my experience of God from my efforts to think about God because faith cannot be isolated from intelligence. What would be the advantage in acting as if I did not know God in order to think more objectively about the nature of my belief? That would be like trying to understand a close friend by pretending that I could temporarily suspend my feelings, affection and memories, indeed, as if I could suspend the relationship itself.

It may be, of course, that the way we start thinking about God is misdirected. We tend to begin by looking for evidence in our experience that there really is a God, and if we manage to locate enough resonance of mystery in our experience, then (we tell ourselves) our faith will have some "proof" to rest upon. The trouble is that we can never be sure enough.

If the way we are thinking about God leads us to raise questions which could never be definitively answered unless God were to stand directly before us and explain what we have been puzzling over, then we are probably asking the wrong questions. We may be raising questions with the idea that in a well-ordered world the act of believing would no longer be necessary: If only we had evidence, proof and certainty, then we could dispense with believing altogether. We would be able to see everything clearly. According to this attitude, faith is not a perfection and a blessing, but a defect. "Blessed are those who have not seen and yet have believed" (Jn 20:29) is turned around to "More blessed are they who believe because they have been privileged to see." Which is not exactly what the evangelist says. For John there are two kinds of believing, believing with seeing and believing without seeing. What is absolutely essential for touching the risen Jesus is believing, and the quality of seeing is what is at stake. People can see without believing; that is, they can lay eyes on the physical presence of Jesus and still not see in him the mystery of God. They are not changed because of their contact with Jesus, as the gospel stories about Jesus' encounters with the scribes and Pharisees abundantly attest. Faith, in other words, is an ingredient of the seeing that counts. Since to see is to know, according to the evangelist, we could say that faith is an essential condition of real knowledge, that is, of knowledge which makes a difference for the way we live. The blessing which Jesus pronounces applies to those whose seeing is informed by faith, and such faith, of course, is the Father's gift.

The development of genuine freedom would never take place unless men and women learned how to believe and to trust. Each of us would remain stunted in our growth toward being fully human unless we developed that spiritual feature which makes us what we are, namely, our freedom. Freedom will not develop, however, unless we learn to trust one another and to make that trusting surrender of ourselves to God, which is the meaning of faith. God did not fashion human beings with intelligence only to tie up our minds with doubts and intellectual knots so that we could never understand those things in life which mattered most! Rather, God has created us in such a way that our minds do not live and grow without faith; faith is essential to the full flowering of human freedom.

Faith takes various forms depending upon what sorts of things people believe. On a very simple level, faith and reason do not happen separately; no human mind survives without belief. We believe our teachers, textbooks, the research of reputable scholars, evening news broadcasts, and so on. Sometimes belief proves to be unfounded, yet by and large one has to agree that human knowledge would make little progress unless people trusted what others have learned or discovered. The mind has to make its act of faith.

There is a deeper level to human faith. No friendship, no love relationship would mature unless people were willing to trust the words and actions of their friends. Absolute certainty of another's affection and good will cannot be guaranteed in this life. Anyone who constantly looked for and demanded proofs of another person's love would find his or her personal relationships crumbling under the weight of doubt, suspicion, jealousy and mistrust. The heart has to make its act of faith too. Furthermore, human beings also have to learn how to trust the universe, to believe that human existence is meaningful and worthwhile. Otherwise we would never feel at home on the earth and at one with creation. The human spirit has to make its own act of faith, believing that human existence owes its origin to reason and heart and not to blindly moving cosmic process.

In short, every life situation includes large elements of believing, for to believe is an eminently reasonable thing for human beings to do. Faith and reason may be distinguishable, but they come together in the natural movement of the human mind. According to some Christian thinkers, believing in Jesus Christ completes the natural orientation of our minds, hearts and spirits toward faith and thus toward the fullest realization of human freedom.

There has to be a consistency between reason and faith. After all, God created human intelligence and everything else besides. God created the possibility of revelation, and God creates the fact of revelation. Revelation comes from God just as human minds and hearts do. In fact, God created Jesus, as well as the history of the Jewish people which preceded him and thus made his birth possible. Since the time of the earliest Christian thinkers and writers, there have been theologians convinced that all of creation speaks to us about God, though all things do not speak in the same way or with the same force. What the mind grasps by reasoning and what it grasps by faith are thus linked because a single divine intention pervades creation, giving the world its meaning and beauty. And God's intention is to be in communion with fragile creatures like us. Faith is not so much a matter of assenting to truths about another world or the afterlife. No, faith is much more a matter of looking at this world and discovering in it the merciful closeness of God. "The kingdom of God," Jesus said, "does not come visibly, nor will people say, 'Here it is,' or 'There it is,' because the kingdom of God is within you" (Lk 17:20-21). The notions of reason and revelation, while distinct, are interrelated. The only cause for wonder is why some people let their lives be taken over by the revelation of the mystery of God while others do not.

Coming to grasp the interrelation of reason and faith can be compared to developing a proficiency in language. Syntax, grammar, vocabulary and accents must be mastered, but the only way to appreciate a language fully is from inside the language—reading it, writing it and speaking it. If one is content only to learn the grammar, one will never understand the language. And this would be unfortunate, for God is the true conversation partner of the human race. The authentic development of the human being includes the growth of a person into faith, that is, into a person who thinks and prays, reasons and believes, discerns and loves. One learns how to read, to write and to speak the language of human living, which is the language of faith. Indeed, I would argue that prayer is what human beings do when they think about life. God is the "You" to whom we inwardly, silently and often unknowingly speak whenever life teases our minds to think seriously and profoundly about things which truly matter.

There is a way of thinking about God which does not throw faith and revelation into even a temporary suspension from reason, a way which is roughly that of St. Anselm and many early Christian writers. Theirs is hardly the only way to begin reflecting about God, but it is an alternative. Rather than starting to think about God by discussing the limits of natural reason and what the mind comes to know about God without the assistance of revealed truths, or by explaining and defending the act of faith by which theological reflection is initiated, suppose we started right in the middle of the experience of being a believer. After all, it is not imperative that we figure out the technical meaning of the notion of revelation, or that we determine precisely whether, in thinking about God, the mind is operating in a natural mode or whether it is being assisted by the light of the Spirit. But it is extremely important that we understand what actually happens to men and women who believe in God, for what happens to them pertains directly to the process of revelation. And here I would call attention to several things.

First, people who believe in God are transformed by their faith into human beings who are lovers in the best sense of the word. Secondly, many people who grow in God discover a kind of darkness overtaking their thoughts about God. Images and words with which they have been familiar lose their capacity to express what is going on inside their hearts and minds. They find it difficult to

distinguish knowing God from not-knowing God. These people do
not actually doubt God's existence, but they may find it meaning-
less to speak about God's existence. Somehow in the very act of
speaking about God, words distance the mind from what it knows
more surely in a non-verbal, non-expressible way.

The darkening of the mind—to draw for a moment on the
imagery of writers like Gregory of Nyssa and the author of *The
Cloud of Unknowing*—is like the crippling of reason that one
experiences when trying to settle why God should be believed in at
all. There is a stumbling block which prevents the mind from
sliding smoothly from natural knowledge to faith. And as I pointed
out, that blockage arises primarily from the way the problem has
been conceived. We cannot slip from reason to faith because reason
and faith do not happen separately. Why? Because we are already
"in" God from the outset, even though many people remain
unaware of the mystery which encloses them. We ought not to
imagine God as being beyond the human world, outside our minds
and hearts, waiting for us to invent or discover reasons for God's
existence. If such were the case, no one would ever arrive at
knowledge of God, natural or otherwise. Instead, the mind must
already be in God. At the moment of grace we see how close, how
all embracing the mystery of God is. The language of prayer may
talk about God coming to us; we ask God to incline an ear, to look
on us with kindness, to draw near and touch us. But God does not
move; God is always here, always attentive and ever seeing. We are
the ones who become aware of God, who learn how to see and
hear the holy mystery; we are the ones who come close. The
reason why some people believe in God and others do not has little
to do with the process of reasoning, but it has much to do with
spirituality.

Three Situations of Faith

For a number of years, I would occasionally find myself imagining that I was on a ship which was sailing over a vast ocean. In the
image, God was the ocean and I was a passenger safely stowed
aboard. When the waves grew too high or the seas too rough, I
could retreat below deck. Or I might be driving a car through a

storm, and God would be the elements raging outside. To protect myself against the wind and rain I had only to roll up the window. Or I might be on a plane. God was the open space outside me, and my journey through time could be described as the story of my passing through God. Whatever storms society was passing through, I could retreat into the security of the church. When the storms of protest and renewal struck the church, I could find refuge in my religious community. And when my religious community was buffeted by the various crises which hit both church and state in the Vietnam and post-Vatican II era, I could retreat into myself and try to rely upon my own resources. But there was no safe harbor there either.

The images were appealing, but they proved wildly off the mark. There is no way of escaping the signs of the times, the events and circumstances of our point in history; God speaks through them. The images needed to be turned inside out. We do not pass through God—or, for that matter, through life—like ships passing over the sea, or planes through the air, or cars through a storm. Rather, it is the living God who passes through us. God is making a journey through human hearts and minds. Sometimes God's presence leaves us confident and consoled; at other times it leaves us exhausted or fearful. God's passing can tear across the layers of our minds like the prow of a ship cutting into the waves. After all, how can we roll up the windows of our souls against the unrelenting pressure of God's passing through our lives? There is no escape from the mystery which we are, and there is no protection against that other mystery which wants to fashion us into its image and likeness.

The mind's challenge, therefore, is learning how to think about God from *inside* our experience of God.

Three descriptive categories helped me to assemble, more or less precisely, some of the major ingredients of religious experience. There are prophets, there are lovers, and there are pilgrims. I do not mean to suggest that each Christian will fall neatly into one of these three categories; human experience resists such tight defini- tion. A person generally manifests elements from each of these categories, if not at the same time, then at different stages of his or her spiritual life. Still, Christians can be identified in terms of one of these groups insofar as their experience approaches that of the prophet, the lover (or mystic) or the pilgrim. The church learns more about the mystery of God through the lives of the prophets, the lovers and the pilgrims among us because God moves within their experience. They are living sacraments, flesh and blood signs of what it is like to live uncovered to the eyes of God. They are men and women who have been drawn out of hiding into the freedom of the children of God.

Who are these people? The experience of a prophetic Christian is unusual, striking, but not necessarily rare. We tend to label as prophets those who bear dramatic witness to their beliefs, people who expose themselves to ridicule, rejection, imprisonment or death for the sake of gospel values, that is to say, for the sake of authentically human values such as freedom, peace, justice or human rights. Like the prophets of the Old Testament their experience often represents an intersection of religion and politics. They find themselves sharply at odds with aspects of their society and culture, and their critique and outrage are strikingly expressed both in words and deeds. Prophetic witness is welcome and necessary for it snaps sleepy and unchallenged believing to attention. It is one clear sign of the Spirit's presence in the world.

Jesus expected his disciples to bear witness to what they believe. Being called upon to testify to their faith by words and by example follows upon their acknowledging Jesus as Lord. But the prophetic Christian also brings a further dimension to religious witness. The Old Testament prophets provide stunning illustrations of this dimension for they not only call attention to injustice and infidelity in their society, they also force us to notice the quality and the intensity of God's own experience.

In his study of the Old Testament prophets, Abraham Heschel suggested that there are two basic forms of prophetic sympathy. The prophet feels with God, that is, he feels what God is experiencing; and he also feels for God.[5] The prophet's anger over political or economic injustice and religious infidelity discloses the depth of divine feeling. The God who called the nation of Israel into existence is outraged and angry with the people, and the prophet makes them keenly aware of that fact. But the prophet also shows sympathy for God. He is saddened or disappointed because God's people have turned faithless and ungrateful, or the prophet feels confident and hopeful when God has been moved by pity and love.

The prophets, then, are people who have been summoned to share in God's experience. Participation in that experience deepens their existence; their lives dramatize a particular feature of God's own way of experiencing the world. Indeed, they bear witness to what they believe and to the depth of their feeling, sometimes to the extent of laying down their lives. The prophet demonstrates what human living is like when it is intensified by divine feeling. That is what renders the burning words of an Amos or Hosea so unforgettable, or the maternal imagery of Isaiah so reassuring. What frightens us in a text like this one is the prospect that God might really be addressing us:

> "I hate, I despise your religious feasts;
> I cannot stand your assemblies.
> Even though you bring me burnt offerings
>   and grain offerings,
> I will not accept them.
> Though you bring me choice fellowship offerings,
> I will have no regard for them.
> Away with the noise of your songs!
> I will not listen to the music of your harps"
> (Am 5:21-23).

What attracts us back to other texts is our hope that the prophet truly reflects what God feels:

> "Can a mother forget the baby at her breast
> and have no compassion on the child she has borne?
> Though she may forget,
> I will not forget you!
> See, I have engraved you on the palms of my hands.
>
> As a mother comforts her child,
> so will I comfort you" (Is 49:15-16; 66:13).

The brilliant witness of prophetic Christians boldly living out their commitment to the gospel arrests our attention. It is unfortunate, however, that they do not always capture our imaginations as well. We are not easily led from admiring their example to penetrating their experience in order to learn what God is like. For prophetic Christians are those who experience in their own souls both the range and the depth of God's feeling for the world. Their feeling for God—for Jesus—is like the feeling one friend has for another. If we want to think about God, therefore, one place to start is from the experience of the friends of God.

The second category is that of the lover. There are some men and women whose lives can be described as stories of being in love with God. One might prefer to call them mystics, but the word *mystic* often summons up too many fuzzy notions about God. Indeed, great mystery surrounds God. Karl Rahner has written of the "incomprehensible mystery of God," "the holy mystery," but there is nothing intrinsically obscure about God. Mystics often speak about a certain darkness that covers the soul and its thoughts as a person ascends the holy mountain which is the divine presence. But the trait which most meaningfully and adequately describes the experience which mystics share is love, and so I refer to them as lovers.

Such people are madly in love with God, and they have grown into the realization that God has been madly in love with them. Their hearts have no other desire than to be possessed by the love they cannot control. Their living dramatizes and intensifies the basic desire for life which is implanted in every human being. But whereas the lives of most of us become confused about what exactly we want or what we are really living for, the lover leaves no room for doubt that only one love truly matters. Lovers do not ignore their neighbors, nor do they devote themselves to serving their brothers and sisters merely to prove their love for God. They know, often implicitly, that God is not like another person who exists alongside everyone else. God is the holy mystery pervading everything we do, touch, think about and hope for. The lover has not encountered a God who competes with human beings for time and affection, nor does the lover reduce human beings to means by which love for God is demonstrated. God is altogether different. God is what a person knows from being fully in love. The "object" of that love is personal, pervasive and inclusive. It is personal without being absorbed by one individual being, not even by a Being that is supreme. It is pervasive and cannot be switched on and off depending on the lover's mood or inner disposition. It is inclusive and incapable of being restricted only to certain people; the lover knows neither enemies nor strangers, only friends. The lover recognizes all as brothers and sisters.

As a person steps ever more deeply into the experience of loving God and of knowing that inexplicable goodness wherein God loves us, the whole of life looks and feels rich with possibilities, ever fresh, unified, even transparently holy. The situation in which he or she lives precludes any thinking about God which might isolate reason from faith, ideas from life, nature from grace. The situation of being in love lends a coherency to thought; it confers unity and wholeness on daily life. One sees integrally in a world where there are reasons, but where reason does not speak the final word, for the final word is love. Reasons are merely the words by which a lover manages to greet the holy mystery of God and to embrace it.

Once again, people who are in love with God have much to teach us about what God is like. For some, God is an idea to be researched and analyzed; for others, God is an experience whose import bursts through the limits of ordinary language. If God does exist, we would do better to listen to the friends of God if we want to learn about the holy mystery which has permeated their lives. If we are unsure whether God exists, then we shall solve nothing by analyzing the coherency of the idea of God. Our only recourse is to reflect upon our own experience: Do we love? Is it a thoroughgoing love? Is it restricted to a few, or does it grow increasingly inclusive? Does it help us to regard the world and our existence as a gift? Does it seek communion with others above everything else? If we can answer questions like these affirmatively, then we are already in

the situation of being in love. We are already in the presence of the
holy mystery, a fact which we should not forget when we set our
minds to thinking about God.

Finally, there is the category of the pilgrim. Real lovers exist,
but most of us are probably not such zealous lovers that our lives
turn into dramatic expressions of being in love with God. We
would probably describe the situation in which we find ourselves in
a humbler way. "Blessed are those whose strength is in you, who
have set their hearts on pilgrimage," wrote the psalmist (Ps 84:5).
And the Sufi saint, Sharafuddin Maneri, observed: "Even though
he may not be able to travel to Mecca, a believer who has prayed
has also gone on a pilgrimage." We are pilgrims, men and women
slowly making our way along the journey of faith. We love, but our
loving still needs a lot of growing up and purifying. We trust God,
but not with the absolute confidence which comes from having
allowed God the freedom to love and accept us even in our sinfulness. We bear witness to the religious values that we cherish, but
without the intensity and singlemindedness of the prophetic
witness. We are pilgrims, and the situation in which our thinking
about God unfolds is affected by a certain dullness of understanding, hesitation and suspicion, and an appetite for reasons and
proofs. We should be consoled by the example of Jesus' first disciples, for they were often just as slow to believe, quick to forget, and
as likely to misunderstand as we are.

For most of us, therefore, thinking about God does not start
with coolly and objectively weighing the reasons for God's existence and pondering the notion of God supplied to us by history,
or philosophy, or theology, or common sense. Thinking about God
proceeds from the situation of our being pilgrims. We have to look
at the whole life-context in which our thinking takes place. Part of
that context includes some measure of doubting and uncertainty. It
also includes our sinfulness, our tendency toward self-centering and
self-serving thinking and acting, and our desire for the things we
hope and dream about. The context from which our thinking
about God begins also embraces our memories, our past and

present experience, the level of our freedom and maturity, and so on.

Thinking does not unfold in isolation from the total context in which human beings find themselves. I have described that situation as basically oriented toward goodness, freedom and life, but also as incomplete, as prone to a certain hardness of heart, as searching and as needing assistance from a believing human community. That community understands itself as embarked upon an historical journey of faith. From its own experience it knows the pitfalls and illusions that can distract people along the way, but it also knows that the direction of its journeying is toward the holy mystery of God. In short, most of us begin our thinking about God primarily as pilgrims, not as men and women whose lives will be spent in a classroom. We may be students, or teachers, or philosophers, or scientists, or parents, but we are first of all men and women on a journey.

I remarked at the beginning of this chapter that accenting the distinction between reason and faith does not appear to yield any practical results. I hope that the point has become clear during the course of this reflection on the experience of being a believer. The distinction between faith and reason dates from the earliest Christian thinkers when they stated that God's coming to us in Jesus was God's free gift, necessary for our salvation, and yet that this gift is anticipated by our native ability to hear God's word of grace. Eventually the distinction appears to have centered on what the mind on its own could know about God, and the earlier emphasis on grace was clouded by the discussion of natural and revealed truths, what could be known about God naturally and what could only be known through a supernatural enlightening by grace.

Once we adopt this way of thinking and speaking, it becomes easy to overlook the fact that real knowledge of God is impossible without some degree of faith. That may explain why there does not seem to be a universally compelling argument for the existence of God: There is no way to prove satisfactorily and definitively that God, the ultimate referent of religious discourse, actually exists. Yet the basic question should not be, Does God exist? The basic question should be, How do people become aware of God's presence? To ask if God exists reduces God to an object which lies outside of us, beyond our world. When reason operates apart from faith, the mind represents God as an object or a notion which can be spoken about, examined and analyzed in a detached, scientific way. But sooner or later the mind is forced to abandon its efforts and concede that the attempt to demonstrate God's existence is no more successful than, say, searching for unicorns. Until you see one, you won't be sure that they actually exist.

Christians think and speak about God, of course, because God—the actual God—has been revealed to us as personal, as the Father of our Lord Jesus Christ. But we cannot allow God to fall into our language as a mere concept around which the mind wraps itself. We must not detach God from our experience, from the total situation in which we come to know ourselves, by letting God become a notion or an abstraction. Human reason was in, of and toward God before theologians ever learned to distinguish reason from faith. The human mind is enclosed by the mystery of God from the start. In fact, being enclosed by the mystery of God is what makes the mind what it is. This is a central Christian insight. There is no way of thinking about human being, or about God—in fact, no possibility for thinking whatsoever—without presupposing divine grace. As von Balthasar writes: "Christian existence is demonstrated and proven as an existence that 'rings true' because it is an existence in faith, which is to say in the continuous act of surrender to him who has first surrendered himself to us."[6]

The fact that we have been loved by God is not merely an item of pious information for religiously minded people. If it is the case that we have been loved by God and that only God's loving us accounts for the way we are, then this fact will reach into every dimension of being human, *whether we realize it or not*. It falls to theologians to describe what a human person is in such a way that it remains clear to all of us that no other fact does full justice to who and what we are. Finally, theology comes to the assistance of spirituality in confirming the experience which knows God to be a lover.

The Spirituality of Christian Thinking

Reflection about God proceeds most fruitfully when it is carried on from within our religious experience. This is simply a matter of respecting the way human knowing occurs. It does not make sense to bracket religion when trying to understand what it means to be human any more than it would make sense to suspend our humanness when trying to understand what it means to be religious. Reason and revelation, being human and being religious, have to happen together. In the laboratory-like conditions of a theology seminar, for example, a considerable amount of bracketing takes place. The same kind of unreality can invade the atmosphere of a retreat or damage the quality and integrity of Christian prayer. For the day-to-day lives of men and women are already enclosed by the mystery of God. Theology can help them to notice that mystery, to describe how it makes itself felt, and to relocate their minds and hearts with respect to the presence of God. But theology does not make the mystery of God present the way a magician springs a rabbit from his hat. Theology only attends to and articulates what is already there.

Religious knowing presupposes situations of faith, and I have related three experiential situations—the prophet's, the lover's and the pilgrim's, although there surely are others. I do not mean to exclude the mind from having its own kind of experience. After all, that is what theology represents, namely, the experience of the theologian's mind. Thinking too can be experienced, and genuine thinking does for the mind what long distance running does for the heart.

Thinking is not daydreaming. It is not idle speculation. It is not a matter of giving free rein to our doubts or continually feeding on our own bright ideas. Genuine thinking puts us in touch with the axis of our inner world. As the 20th-century philosopher Martin Heidegger put it, genuine thinking plows furrows into the soil of Being. Genuine thinking proceeds from an encounter with our own spirit, and it leads us to recognize that fuller Spirit in which all human beings share. Without that Spirit we would have no stories to tell, no history to record, no possibility for hoping that we are even now being drawn by a power which transcends all the words and images we use to describe who we are.

Mind is a metaphor for the whole human person, of course. But the term denotes the intellectual side of our being—our thinking, our questioning, our supposing, our doubting, our judging and deciding, even our believing. The mind has its own experience. It seizes upon, or is captured by, thoughts which aggravate its existence and carve deep lines into its knowledge, thoughts which chart the course of the mind's ascent to God. The mind has its way of loving. It shows affection for ideas, relishes clarity and yet is soothed by mystery. By "standing underneath" things, the mind becomes the place where the world displays itself in order to delight our sensibilities and intrigue our imaginations. The mind loves and, as St. Augustine observed in his work on the Trinity, it especially loves being a mind.

The mind also engages upon its own kind of journey. It experiences the burden of ignorance, the thirst for understanding, the humiliation of having spent time thinking over things which are not worth knowing, the joy of discovery, the satisfaction of being united with what it has spent years attempting to understand. In short, the mind exhibits a spiritual life of its own. Genuine thinking is the mind's way of praying.

In the course of this chapter I have not adverted to the distinction sometimes drawn between faith and belief. Many people would readily grant the fact that human beings have to learn how to believe or trust one another, but they would posit a strong difference between faith of this sort and faith in God. So would I. They would argue that we cannot come to faith in God unless God first draws us by grace, and so would I. But whereas they would prefer to talk about natural faith and supernatural faith, I prefer to see both forms as connected, as two moments on a trajectory, as varying by degrees of comprehensiveness without any radical disjunction. One moves from the visible world to the world of things which are real but not immediately visible. Even here, however, I think it is necessary to exercise caution. Believing in God is much different from believing a textbook or the word of our teachers and friends.

This difference has to be measured in terms of the kind of person we become insofar as we are believers. One form of belief makes people intelligent and reasonable, for believing is a natural and reasonable human response to the world. The other form of belief makes people religious and opens the possibility for further personal transformation and development as they become increasingly conscious of the presence of God. The point I have insisted upon in this chapter is that the mind is already in God from the moment it first begins to wonder, to think, to raise questions or to believe. Even so-called natural faith (which functions in everyday life and without which we would learn nothing about the world) is rooted in God. For those who believe in God, I have urged, thinking about God cannot leave faith in parentheses, any more than we can think about the nature of motherhood while suspending everything we have become as a result of the way in which our own mothers have influenced and shaped us.

Our minds exist in situations of faith, as we have already seen. I think Carlo Carretto speaks to some of the concerns we have been considering when he writes:

> The catechism is not enough, theology is not enough, formulas are not enough to explain the Unity and Trinity of God. We need loving communication, we need the presence of the Spirit. That is why I do not believe in theologians who do not pray, who are not in humble communication of love with God. Neither do I believe in the existence of any human power to pass on authentic knowledge of God. Only God can speak about Himself, and only the Holy Spirit, who is love, can communicate this knowledge to us. When there is a crisis in the Church, it is always here: a crisis of contemplation.[7]

Above all, the church is a situation of faith, a place where our minds come into contact with the mystery of God. By *place* I do not mean a building, not even solely a social or cultural institution. The church is not sacraments and scripture, hierarchy and cult, devotional practices and moral teachings. The church includes

these things, to be sure; they form its visible aspect. Primarily,
however, the church is the community of believers throughout the
ages who have been called to know and follow Jesus, who have at
least tried to be faithful disciples, and who have joined themselves—their hearts as well as their minds—to Jesus in his dying and
rising. If people manage to find God, despite the human weakness
and limitations to which the church in every generation is subject,
within the community of believers, among men and women who
are gradually making their way toward God, then this indeed is
mystery. For mystery is something to marvel at. Mystery is what
astonishes the mind and excites the heart without ever proving or
exhausting itself. Or, to use St. Thomas' phrase, mystery curbs
presumption. It awakens us to fresh meaningfulness, to depths
within everyday things, of which we had been unaware.

But mystery does not expose itself. It never fully uncovers the
ground of our hope, of our faith, of our love. We hope, but we do
not ultimately know why. We believe, but we are often at a loss to
explain why, finally, anyone should be a believer. We love, but we
have no way of accounting for why the ultimate reasonableness of
life and existence in this world should be located in love. What
would it profit us to gain the whole world, if we never experienced
love and never learned how to return it? Mystery arouses our hearts
and minds to ponder and to embrace the hidden ground of meaning and life. Just as we grasp that the ocean has a bottom even
though we cannot see it, so too perhaps we grasp that life has an
inner ground which remains hidden. Otherwise, there would be no
surface—no lasting meaning, no life or hope or love in the first
place. Do people today still touch this mystery in the church, the
situation of their faith? I think they do.

FOOTNOTES

1. St. Thomas Aquinas, *Summa Contra Gentiles*, Book 1, chapter 5, no.
   4, and chapter 7, no. 2, trans. Anton C. Pegis (Notre Dame, IN:
   University of Notre Dame Press, 1975), pp. 70, 74.

2. Vatican II, "Dogmatic Constitution on Divine Revelation," no. 2.

3. Hans Urs von Balthasar, *The Glory of the Lord*, vol. 1, *Seeing the Form*, trans. Erasmo Leivka-Merikakis (Edinburgh: T. & T. Clark, 1982), p. 146.

4. Edward Hardy, ed., *Christology of the Later Fathers* (Philadelphia: Westminster Press, 1954), p. 110.

5. Abraham J. Heschel, *The Prophets*, vol. 2 (San Francisco: Harper & Row, 1962).

6. Von Balthasar, op. cit. p. 227.

7. Carlo Carretto, *The God Who Comes*, trans. Rose Mary Hancock (Maryknoll, N.Y.: Orbis Books, 1974), p. 78.

CHAPTER 3

The Religious Experience of Jesus' Disciples

"Father, I want those you have given me to be with me where I am, and to see my glory."

—John 17:24

What is more, I consider everything a loss compared to the surpassing greatness of knowing Christ Jesus my Lord, for whose sake I have lost all things. I consider them rubbish, that I may gain Christ.

—Philippians 3:8

We have been approaching the idea of revelation from the perspective of spirituality and experience. Revelation, I have suggested, can be regarded as the process of our learning how to live in the presence of God—a God who uncovers us to ourselves, a God who journeys through our minds and hearts, who moves within our actions and desires, our memories and our dreams. Some people might still prefer, however, to define revelation in terms of its conceptual or informational content. They would urge that the content of revelation is Jesus Christ and the God whom Jesus addresses as Father, the God who is manifested in Jesus' life and ministry, his death and resurrection. Yet if we squeeze this definition for its practical consequences, don't we have to admit sooner or later that Jesus is not only known about but also experienced? And then should we not go on to ask, What did the disciples experience as they came to know Jesus? How was their living affected by being his followers?

In this chapter I shall propose twelve aspects of that experience. They can help us to grasp a bit more firmly the pattern of living which we too might expect to experience once we have been drawn out of hiding into companionship with Jesus.

The Relationship Between Jesus and His Disciples

When the disciples approached Jesus with the request that he teach them how to pray, perhaps they were not merely approaching their rabbi for the words of a new prayer. After all, they already had prayers which they could say to God, particularly the psalms. They could probably recite a number of the psalms by heart, and they surely knew the great *Shema* prayer which every devout Jew would have said in the morning and again in the evening: "Hear, O Israel: The LORD our God, the LORD is one. Love the LORD your God with all your heart and with all your soul and with all your strength" (Dt 6:4-5).

Although Luke portrays Jesus as answering the disciples' request by giving them the Lord's Prayer, I think we are on safe grounds in assuming that these words are meant to summarize the spirit of Jesus' teaching. The prayer emerges from Jesus' own faith, his own religious experience. I would be surprised to discover that the disciples were simply interested in learning another formula for prayer, since there is so much more to learning how to pray than memorizing a fixed set of words. And even though the prayer begins with "Father," it seems unlikely that the disciples were searching for a new name for God. They already knew how to address God. Rather, the word *Father* stands for the whole range of Jesus' experience of God. *Father* abbreviates Jesus' faith, his way of regarding the world, his attitude toward other men and women, how he views himself in relation to God, the particular feeling out of which he prays and reads scripture. It is Jesus' experience of God which stands behind his parables and stories, his sermons and healings, and his relationships with others, whether with his disciples, the tax collectors and public sinners, the scribes and Pharisees, or with friends like Martha and Mary or the Twelve whom he personally chose as special companions. When he tells his disciples to say "Father," Jesus is inviting them to know God as he knows God. He is inviting them to share in his religious experience.[1]

However much the disciples participated in Jesus' religious experience, they never regarded him simply as another messenger of God. They did not receive his teaching and then relegate him to his place in history as a first-century agent of divine communication. The disciples did not look upon him as someone who brought new knowledge or information about God which could have been delivered by any number of prophets or inspired preachers. Jesus not only introduced his disciples into a new experience of God; that experience was inseparable, as the disciples only fully realized after the resurrection, from their being with Jesus. This is such an elementary point that students of Christian faith often miss it.

Jesus played an indispensable role in the new experience of God to which the disciples were being introduced. As one contemporary New Testament scholar writes:

> In the end of the day the religious experience of the Christian is not merely like that of Jesus, it is experience which at all characteristic and distinctive points is derived from Jesus the Lord, and which only makes sense when this derivative and dependent character is recognized.[2]

Thus, the experience of the disciples would not be totally like that of Jesus. The gospel of John, for example, could still record Jesus as saying, "my Father and your Father . . . my God and your God" (Jn 20:17). A dependency seems to be implied here. The disciples depend upon Jesus for their knowledge and experience of God, and *they will always be depending on him* for this. Jesus enables them to live in the presence of the God whom he knows, by whom he has been loved and missioned, the one whom he has obeyed even to death, the one to whom he prayed and about whose kingdom he preached, the one who sent him to men and women in order to forgive their sins and to "take away the sin of the world" (Jn 1:29). Jesus was not just another in a line of teachers and prophets; he was not simply a holy man or a charismatic preacher and healer. Jesus was the one in whom the Spirit of God dwelled in a particular way, a way so special that the early communities would search for appropriate titles which would illuminate and underscore his uniqueness. Jesus was Lord, Savior, the Anointed One (Messiah, Christ), the Lamb of God, the Son of God, God's Word-made-flesh.

The disciples did not arrive at these conclusions all at once.

They grew in their knowledge of Jesus, just as Jesus had grown in his knowledge of God. The gospels were written some 30 to 60 years after the original events which they narrate. The resurrection had long since occurred, and those who read or listened to the gospels would already have known the outcome of Jesus' story. (We may overlook this point when we read the gospels today. The outcome was known to the evangelist from the first stroke of his pen. This means that resurrection faith governed the telling of the whole story.) Only after the resurrection and the giving of the Spirit did the first disciples begin to draw the complete picture. By then they could comprehend somewhat who Jesus was, what he had done, what his ministry of healing and forgiving sins was all about. By then they could come to some insight into why Jesus was more than a teacher. They realized, in the wake of their dreadful flight and fear at the time of Jesus' betrayal and arrest, that before they could ever hope to follow his teaching and imitate his example, Jesus had to do something for them which they could not do for themselves. Only after the cross and resurrection did the disciples fathom how much God had been working in and through Jesus. They would have stood very little chance of following Jesus' instruction, of praying as he had, of forgiving one another as radically and thoroughly as Jesus did, until they understood how Jesus had lived and died *for them*. The Sermon on the Mount, the great examples of service and compassion which Jesus had left them, even perhaps the words of the Lord's Prayer, would simply not have registered their full significance until after the resurrection. Resurrection faith would be the context in which the disciples would remember and tell the story of Jesus and the story of their own lives. After that, they could never think about God apart from Jesus.

The disciples would not have grasped where the nerve of Jesus' teaching lay, nor would they have been able to get inside the mind and heart of Jesus, until his Spirit had been shared with them. But this could not have happened until he had died and was raised to new life. It was the cross which drove home to the disciples the fact that they were sinners, every bit as sinful as the men and women of the forgiveness episodes in Jesus' ministry. The cross had dramatically uncovered their sinfulness; it exposed their cowardice, their pettiness, their hardness of heart, their shame and confusion, and their sorrow. The cross not only drew them out of hiding, a hiding of which they were probably not even fully aware, it also spoke of how much Jesus had loved them. But they would not have been able to hear this word apart from the resurrection. In raising Jesus, God said yes to his ministry. In raising Jesus, God once and for all invested the cross of Jesus with saving power. How did this happen?

I want to avoid speculating on what might have been going on in Jesus' mind during the closing months and hours of his ministry. We simply do not have enough material in the gospels to reward such an effort. Clearly he saw that his mounting confrontation with religious and political authorities was pulling his life more and more into the prophetic pattern, where the prophet's word is rejected and the prophet himself is drawn to his fate. This happens precisely because God has spoken to the prophet, and God's concerns have gradually and irreversibly become mingled with his own life:

> "O Jerusalem, Jerusalem, you who kill the prophets and stone those sent to you, how often I have longed to gather your children together, as a hen gathers her chicks under her wings, but you were not willing" (Mt 23:37).

The word of God which he proclaimed and served assumed a life and momentum of its own in the prophet's actions, testimony and fate.

Jesus surely would have read Isaiah, especially the chapters about God's suffering servant, the one who suffers on behalf of the people. He would have known that sometimes the innocent and the holy are called upon to suffer, even to laying down their lives, in order to take what is sinful and evil away from human society. Not that God demands the death of the just in order to atone for human sin; if some people believe this is the case, then there is something terribly wrong with the way we tell the story of Jesus. But it does happen that goodness can provoke its own destruction

because evil cannot abide it. Sinners often react against goodness
and virtue since the example of the virtuous person keeps reminding the rest of us that we could be different people. The humanity
of a sinner is deformed, and the righteous person is a painful,
humiliating reminder of that fact. Holiness, in other words, chases
sin out of hiding.

But no useful purpose is served in thinking that one is suffering
on behalf of others if others are never aware of it. What advantage
would the suffering and death of Jesus hold, considering that he
believed that he would give his life both for his disciples and "for
many" (an Aramaic expression which has the inclusive sense of
"for all"), if (1) the disciples did not understand why his death was
necessary for them and (2) if "the many" were never aware of who
Jesus was and what he had done? I don't think they would have
automatically identified Jesus as the lamb of sacrifice. The symbol
of the lamb of God *interprets* the dying of Jesus; it is not the reason
for his dying. Nor would the disciples have immediately regarded
Jesus as the suffering servant of the later chapters of the Book of
Isaiah. Again, those passages would help to interpret the death of
Jesus, to attach some significance to it, but they would not supply
the reason for his dying. Why then does Jesus suffer? Why is he
brought to his death?

Jesus died because he was resented, betrayed and hated. He was
killed out of envy, because he threatened certain vested political
interests, because he had taken religion into his own hands. Jesus, a
good and holy person, one who healed and who loved, who
instructed others about God and God's reign in human society and
in human hearts, died. This Jesus was betrayed by human sinfulness. And he consented to letting this happen because there simply
was no other way out of the madness of sin than to give sin its
violent way. Yet this was not the whole story. Jesus was hardly
surrendering to the power of sin. Far from it. He had come to
overturn the reign of sin in the world. No, Jesus was surrendering
to God. He believed—and our faith rests upon Jesus' faith or it rests
on nothing—Jesus *believed* that God would not allow sin to van-
quish his mission to forgive sins and to heal human brokenness and
alienation. And finally, the disciples and the world would have to

notice this man's dying as they would notice no other's because the resurrection made it clear that Jesus had been one with God as no one else had ever been. In short, the early Christian communities would tell the story of Jesus with one important note that the disciples at first could never have grasped. They would say not just that Jesus had died for them, but that there on the cross God had been betrayed and crucified. This was the only way God could convince the world of its real worth.

Jesus believed. He believed that God's sole desire for the world was to give it life, to take away the burden of its sin, and to invite it into the closest and most intimate union with the holy and silent mystery of God's love. Throughout his ministry, Jesus laid bare sin's ragged face. No wonder, then, that sin would either hide from him or attack him. But the raw and fearful presence of evil is also the face of a man or of a woman; it is the human heart spoiled by its dismal refusal to believe that people like us could be infinitely and eternally desirable to God. Yes, I am reading meaning into the event of Jesus' death. Yet unless one meditates on how the cross uncovered the sinfulness of the disciples, one would forever miss why Jesus became essential to their new experience of God.

The followers of Jesus had undoubtedly committed sins before they met him, and they would have asked God for forgiveness many times in their lives. They were believers. They had prayed the penitential psalms, like Psalm 51. Many had probably submitted to the baptism of John, the baptism of repentance. Indeed, in solidarity with them even Jesus had done so. In coming to know Jesus, however, something else happened. Jesus was not only forgiving their faults in God's name, but he was also calling them to live with the freedom of God's children. They were being strangled by sin, and so was the entire human race. There was simply no way out of sure, slow death at the hands of sin except to experience the holy mystery of God as Jesus had. The God of Jesus was love, compassionate closeness, mercy, freedom and life. That God was "Abba, Father." That God loved human beings even though they are sinful, and this was the momentous truth which awaited the death and resurrection of Jesus for its definitive illustration. For after being raised, Jesus continued to do what he had done before his death. He assured his disciples of peace. By eating with them, he re-set the example of companionship, of mercy and compassion, of reconciliation and acceptance, which all the meals of his public ministry demonstrated. With the resurrection Jesus charged his disciples to forgive sins in his name. From Peter he elicited a deep profession of love and thereby reassured Peter of his affection and his unchanged desire to have Peter be in his company.

If the resurrection signified nothing else, it would certainly underline the central role of forgiveness and reconciliation in Jesus' ministry. With the resurrection the whole story of Jesus has become the sign or symbol of God's unbreakable love for the human race, no matter how wretched or ingrained its sinfulness. But who will tell the world about this? Who will tell the story of Jesus and bear witness to God's merciful closeness? Who will dare the world to confront its hardness of heart, even at the risk of enduring rejection, contempt, humiliation and perhaps death? The disciples of Jesus dared this because to have experienced God's love as Jesus had, to have experienced the crucified and risen Jesus as still forgiving, still calling them to faith, is to have experienced themselves as sent into the world to carry on the ministry of Jesus. From then on the chief business of the disciples would be forgiving sins in Jesus' name:

> He told them, "This is what is written: The Christ will suffer and rise from the dead on the third day, and repentance and forgiveness of sins will be preached in his name to all nations, beginning at Jerusalem" (Lk 24:46-47).

> "He commanded us to preach to the people and to testify that he is the one whom God appointed as judge of the living and the dead. All the prophets testify about him that everyone who believes in him receives forgiveness of sins through his name" (Acts 10:42-43).

> Again Jesus said, "Peace be with you! As the Father has sent me, I am sending you." And with that he breathed on them and said, "Receive the Holy Spirit. If you

forgive anyone his sins, they are forgiven; if you do not
forgive them, they are not forgiven" (Jn 20:21-23).

"If you forgive": Not just by reciting a formula or making the sign
of the cross, but by doing what Jesus did. Talk with people about
the things of God. Spend time with them. Let them tell you their
stories. Sit at table and eat with them. If they have offended you,
hold no grudge. Pray to the Father on their behalf. Touch and hold
them. Convince them of God's loving acceptance by all you do
and all that you are. "If you do not forgive": If you are not there, if
you do not go out to them, if you remain locked behind closed
doors for fear of being hurt or for fear of losing your undisturbed
peace of soul, then they will never hear the word of forgiveness. No
one will bring it to them. "If you do not forgive": This is not a
condition, as if to imply that in some cases the community might
withhold forgiveness. It is a statement of fact that without you,
forgiveness will not happen. Without the disciples of Jesus, the
ministry of forgiving will cease. Since God is the one who forgives
in and through Jesus, the disciples must make Jesus present through
their preaching, their actions, through their being a community of
love—the community of Jesus' disciples.

Before proceeding to examine some aspects of the religious
experience of those who follow Jesus, it might be helpful to pause
for a brief meditation on the difference between praying with Jesus
and praying apart from him. What interests us, after all, is the
spirituality of revelation. To keep our reflection from drifting away
from experience and into the realm of religious concepts, I think it
is important to let our minds feel the significance of being with
Jesus.

Begin by reading Psalm 139 three times, slowly and
meditatively. The first time imagine that Jesus is praying
the psalm, and listen attentively to how the psalm
sounds as he speaks it. Pay close attention to the shifts
of meaning as Jesus recites the verses.

On the second reading, pray the psalm alone. Listen

to yourself speaking the verses, and say them as meaningfully and devoutly as you can.

On the third reading, imagine that Jesus and you are
reciting the psalm together. Imagine that both of you are
making the same prayer.

After completing the third reading, reflect on the
following questions: What did I experience each time I
read the prayer? Which way of reading the psalm would I
like to return to? No matter how privately I might have
prayed in the past, do I still think that the Christian
ever really prays alone? If Jesus is always entering into my
prayer and praying alongside me, am I ever drawn into
his prayer, using his words and praying alongside him?
Who prays my life, who speaks me to God, even when I
am not thinking of God, even if I have wandered far
from God?

Thank God if we can answer that Jesus prays in us,
through us, and for us.

Twelve Features of the Disciples' Experience

The most prominent aspect of the disciples' experience of God
is that, having come to know Jesus, their being with God was
intimately joined to their being with Jesus. This point is absolutely
essential to Christian faith. Even a cursory reading of Paul's letters
should make the point abundantly clear. The gospel of John also
confirms this point. There is no knowing the God who is Father of
Jesus Christ apart from being in the company of Jesus: The disciple
comes to the Father through, with and in Jesus. Christian spirituality obviously centers on Jesus, but it does so only because being
with Jesus centers the disciple's life in the Father. Properly speaking,
then, Christian spirituality is theocentric—God-centering—rather
than Christocentric. Let me elaborate.

The mystery of grace, dynamically at work in the life of the
believer, ultimately leads to the God and Father of our Lord Jesus
Christ. Through Jesus we are led into ever deeper union with God:

"Through him *you believe in God*, who raised him from the dead
and glorified him, and so *your faith and hope are in God*" (1 Pt 1:21,
emphasis added). *Through* Jesus, and not simply *on account of* him,
the believer is joined more closely to God than would be possible
without Jesus. "If anyone loves the world, the love *of the Father* is
not in him" (1 Jn 1:15, emphasis added). It is the Father's love
which has been manifested to the world in Jesus. Consequently the
writer continues, "No one who denies the Son has the Father;
whoever acknowledges the Son has the Father also" (1 Jn 1:23).
The decisive stress falls on the mystery of God—"the God and
Father of our Lord Jesus Christ, the Father of compassion and the
God of all comfort" (2 Cor 1:3). If we are to take possession of the
love which the Father has for us, then we must fulfill the Father's
command:

> To believe in the name of his Son, Jesus Christ, and to
> love one another as he [God] commanded us. Those
> who obey his [God's] commands *live in him* [God], and
> *he* [God] *in them*. And this is how we know he [God]
> lives in us: We know it by the Spirit he gave us (1 Jn
> 3:23-24, emphasis added).[3]

But how can we be sure that we have the Spirit? Because the Spirit
leads us to recognize the full humanity of Jesus. And, as Vatican II
reminds us, those who follow Jesus, the fully human being, become
more human themselves.[4]

This intertwining of Jesus and the mystery of God remains the
central element in the Christian understanding of God. God,
therefore, must always be properly called "the Father of our Lord
Jesus Christ." Knowing the Father in Jesus entails a number of
features which can be collected without too much difficulty from a
careful reading of the New Testament. These features bear upon the
process of revelation because they characterize the experience of
living openly in the presence of God.

1.   The religious experience of the disciples involves community. Being with Jesus sooner or later lands the disciple in the
company of the other men and women for whom Jesus also cares

and whom he likewise is calling to be his followers. The disciple
realizes that a purely private and exclusive relationship with Jesus is
not possible on Jesus' terms. Eventually the disciple prays and
behaves in ways that reflect a growing concern for the wider world,
especially for the ones to whom Jesus himself is partial—the poor,
the powerless, the brokenhearted, the confused sinner, the victims
of injustice or any sort of oppression. This entails developing a
sense of responsibility toward his or her brothers and sisters. It
means being mindful of their physical, human, and spiritual needs.
It means approaching them for forgiveness and acknowledging with
them a common dependence upon Jesus. Hence, as long as there
are men and women who are friends of Jesus there will always be a
community of disciples, the body of Christ, his church. The
uncovering action of God in our midst draws us out of our isolation
and privacy, away from any self-centering relationship with Jesus
and into the community of disciples. God in Christ exposes and
then redeems us from the loneliness of trying to lead our religious
lives by ourselves.

2.   That experience includes *the sense of being a loved sinner*.
The disciple understands the meaning of forgiveness both through
watching Jesus forgive others and by experiencing that forgiveness
personally. What acceptance the men and women around Jesus
must have experienced simply because such a person wanted to be
in their company, and because he called them to be with him! "He
saw a man named Matthew sitting at the tax collector's booth.
'Follow me,' he told him, and Matthew got up and followed him' "
(Mt 9:9). How else might Jesus signify God's merciful closeness
than by sitting at table and breaking bread in the homes of those
whom everyone would recognize as sinners? "While Jesus was
having dinner at Matthew's house, many tax collectors and 'sinners' came and ate with him and his disciples" (Mt 9:10). Such
behavior was bound to provoke criticism, for the tax-collectors were
notoriously dishonest, surely not suitable companions for someone
who claimed God for his Father: "When the Pharisees saw this,
they asked his disciples, 'Why does your teacher eat with tax

collectors and 'sinners'?" (Mt 9:11) Why, indeed, does our Jesus eat with the likes of people like these? Because Jesus was trying to uncover for them the basic truth about us, that we are first and foremost children of God; we may be sinners, but we are deeply loved.

Because of Jesus, the disciple has the knowledge of being loved and accepted by God, the experience of being daily created and renewed through Christ. If this were not so, then it would be hard to explain why the early communities recalled and recorded so many forgiveness stories from Jesus' ministry. A forgiveness story is basically a creation story; it tells of God's fashioning someone anew into the divine image and likeness. Those communities celebrated the Lord's supper in his memory, as he instructed, for he gave his body and blood—that is, his life and his love—so that sins might be forgiven. His instruction to "do this in memory of me" was not spoken because he feared the disciples would forget him. Rather, Jesus knew that unless they continually recalled what he had done, they would soon forget who they were and how valuable they were in the Father's eyes.

3.   Another feature of the experience of the disciples was *a sense of mission*. Jesus had summoned his disciples so that he might send them out:

> Jesus went up into the hills and called to him those he wanted, and they came to him. He appointed twelve—designating them apostles—that *they might be with him* and *that he might send them out to preach* (Mk 3:13-14, emphasis added).

Mission, being sent, is the logical outcome of discipleship, just as for Jesus mission arose from his sense of sonship and his being-with-the-Father. To be with the Father meant being sent to preach the kingdom of God. Mission is implied in resurrection faith since one could not have experienced the risen Jesus without feeling impelled to bear witness:

> That which was from the beginning, which we have heard, which we have seen with our eyes, which we

have looked at and our hands have touched—this we
proclaim concerning the Word of life (1 Jn 1:1).

The conviction that we have a mission to accomplish with our
lives, that we are in this world for a purpose, and that God has
called us into existence for God's sake and not for our own, is a
sign of grace. People who lead their lives out of such conviction, a
conviction which arises from a faith relationship with Jesus, are
charismatic. They have discovered the Spirit's power at work in
their lives. They are people with a sense of mission, faithful to the
teaching and example of Jesus, who daily bear witness to him. Paul
portrays charismatic enthusiasm for Christ and the gospel more
than anyone else in the New Testament. But the fact that all of us
are not St. Pauls does not mean we should be any less enthusiastic
in our witness to Jesus. In whatever circumstances or vocation we
find ourselves, if we are with Jesus then we are people who have
been both called and missioned. Not all disciples are apostles, true,
but every follower of Jesus is sent: "Go home to your family and tell
them how much the Lord has done for you, and how he has had
mercy on you" (Mk 5:19); "The Lord appointed seventy-two others
and sent them two by two ahead of him to every town and place
where he was about to go" (Lk 10:1). There is no place in the
world where Jesus will not go, if only his disciples prepare the way
for him by their witness. To the degree that we take our discipleship seriously, being with Jesus introduces us to the experience of
being called by the Lord and sent into "every town and place,"
every circumstance, profession, neighborhood or situation—every
place—in the world where we would expect Jesus to go.

4.   Another feature is *freedom*. To be with Jesus is to experience the grace of being truly free. Paul wrote of "the glorious
freedom of the children of God" (Rom 8:21), and John records Jesus
as saying, "the truth will set you free" (Jn 8:32). Freedom is a
Spirit-given quality of life and action wherein the disciple is no
longer a slave to fear of any kind, no longer crippled by attach-
ments to money, possessions, security or human respect. Jesus frees
his disciples from their shameful past, like the woman at the well.

He frees them from their anger, as when James and John wanted to call down fire on an unwelcoming village. Jesus frees them from their cowardice, as when he returns to the upper room where the disciples are hiding and breathes the Spirit of peace upon them. Out of such freedom the disciple is ready to be sent and to bear witness to the gospel. The disciple does not serve God out of fear, nor out of a secret wish for special recognition by the Lord, the church, or human society. There are no honorary degrees or civic citations, no cash awards or medals for distinguished service, no feature articles or promotions to ecclesiastical dignities. Evangelical freedom is its own reward. The free disciple can journey with Christ. The free disciple can be poor with Christ. The free disciple can forgive with Christ. The free disciple can suffer and die with Christ.

5. *Empowering trust* is the confidence a disciple has in God which enables the willing and the doing of great things. "I can do everything," Paul writes, "through him who gives me strength" (Phil 4:13). This is first of all true in the example of Jesus. Jesus not only trusted his Father, but that trust made it possible for him to confront opposition, to call ordinary men and women like us to follow him, to cure those afflicted with various diseases, to preach about forgiveness to those who were social and political victims, and to walk into Jerusalem knowing full well the fate he was inviting. He relied solely on his faith in the Father that he would not ultimately be left alone. Jesus could do all things through the Father who strengthened him.

The working of a miracle was not some magical, arcane act. On the contrary, Jesus *trusted* that God would heal through him. Jesus trusted that the Father cares for human beings and that the Father knows how to give good things to those who ask him. Do we trust like that? We should not assume that Jesus knew people would follow him when he called. He had to trust that the Father had missioned him for the work of preaching the kingdom, and he had to trust that there would be some men and women who would open their hearts to his message and follow him. Do we believe that the gospel still has power to move ordinary men and women to lay aside everything in order to follow the teaching and example of Jesus? Do we trust like that? We should not assume that Jesus resigned himself to his fate without much struggle because he knew the outcome. He was not a performer on a stage playing his part and delivering his lines, informed by the Father of everything beforehand. He had to trust God, just as the prophets did or as the people of faith who composed the psalms, which he surely read and upon which he must have meditated. Imagine Jesus praying verses like these:

> For I am poor and needy,
> and my heart is wounded within me. . . .
> My knees give way from fasting;
> my body is thin and gaunt.
> I am an object of scorn to my accusers;
> when they see me they shake their heads.
>
> Help me, O LORD my God;
> save me in accordance with your love.
> Let them know that it is your hand,
> that you, O LORD, have done it.
> They may curse, but you will bless;
> when they attack they will be put to shame,
> but your servant will rejoice.
> My accusers will be clothed with disgrace
> and wrapped in shame as in a cloak.
>
> With my mouth I will greatly extol the LORD;
> in the great throng I will praise him.
> For he stands at the right hand of the needy one,
> to save his life from those who condemn him
> (Ps 109:22-31).

Jesus trusted that his life was in the Father's hands. Do we, his followers, want to trust like that? Do we really want to live such profound surrender to a love whose ways we shall not always understand? Empowering trust does not mean that we will not sink. But if we do—when death eventually comes—God will already be there: "If I make my bed in the depths, you are there" (Ps 139:8). It is, after all, the spirit of Jesus' own trust and faith which resonates through Luke 12 and Matthew 6 where Jesus tells his listeners not to worry or be anxious about food or drink, or about their appearance or their health, or the length of their lives.

Empowering trust also refers to the confidence that Jesus placed in his disciples. Jesus trusted his followers to be his witnesses, to carry to every town and place the gift of the Spirit, to preach the reign of God and to expel the powers of darkness in his name. He trusted that they would know the right things to do and to say because his Spirit was in them. As a result, the disciple too is empowered to do the kind of things Jesus did. The disciple experiences himself or herself as chosen and trusted by the Lord, entrusted with the Lord's own ministry of preaching and forgiving, of teaching others to pray and setting an example of loving service. The disciple too prays through the prophets and the psalms, trusting that the Lord's word will be fulfilled. The disciple experiences the power of Jesus' life and saving death. The disciple knows that despite his or her blindness and sinfulness Jesus will still be there, calling the disciple into his company. As Paul wrote, "But he said to me, 'My grace is sufficient for you, for my power is made perfect in weakness.' . . . For when I am weak, then I am strong" (2 Cor 12:9,10).

6. *Compassion* is the ability to view the world as God sees it. In the story of the Good Samaritan we read that the priest saw the robbers' victim, one of his own countrymen, and he passed by. The Levite saw the victim, and he too passed by. The Samaritan—the outcast—saw the one who had been beaten by the robbers, and he took pity on him. And that is how God sees the world, with compassion. When the disciple learns how to forgive as Jesus did, when the disciple too can forgive his or her enemies, then the disciple has begun to imitate God.

To be with Jesus is to grow in compassion. To know God in Christ is to experience the unfathomable mystery of God's affection for the world. It is to know why divine forgiveness is not a matter of seven times, or even seventy times seven times. Divine forgiveness cannot be measured. It proceeds from such profound compassion that only an insight into the sign of the crucified Jesus will uncover the mystery at the heart of Jesus' experience of God.

7.   Another feature of the disciples' experience is that of being called to *simplicity of life* and evangelical detachment. Both the urgency of Jesus' call to follow him and to bear witness to his teaching, and the very nearness of God's kingdom, demand and call forth a style of being poor. This is not to glamorize or romanticize poverty. Becoming materially poor is only desirable when the disciple is living and working among those who are unwillingly poor and is trying to express his or her solidarity with them for Jesus' sake. A truly poor life embraced out of a profound desire to follow Jesus who became poor for our sake is a sign of inner freedom. Or, to put things another way, the one who is truly free leads an uncluttered existence. Such a person is not preoccupied with making money, dazzled by fashions or seduced by fads. Clearly the truly free person can appear somewhat out of place in a consumer society.

To be with Jesus is to grow in freedom, and being poor—being willing and able to let go of anything which stands between ourselves and the holy mystery of God—is a way of living the freedom of the children of God. There simply is not enough time for the disciple to become preoccupied with concerns which distract him or her from the one thing necessary: following Jesus. To follow him is to have found the pearl of great price, the treasure buried in the field, the well that never runs dry; it is to live out of hiding and, at last, to be free. Luke says the disciples left *everything* and followed Jesus. What would we not lay aside if we could have the one thing we have always wanted, even when we did not realize it? Paul confesses that for the sake of knowing Jesus he has lost all things and counts them as worthless: "I consider everything a loss compared to the surpassing greatness of knowing Christ Jesus my Lord, for whose sake I have lost all things. I count them rubbish, that I may gain Christ and be found in him" (Phil 3:8-9). Turning poor and letting go are necessary if we want to be where Jesus is.

The gospel calls us to prize simplicity and detachment in our living. As far as the gospel is concerned, poverty and freedom belong together. To know God in Christ means turning poor precisely in order to be free.[5]

8. An eighth feature to this experience is the sense of *being on a journey*. Once a person has decided to follow Jesus, then life becomes comparable to a pilgrimage. I adverted to this idea in the last chapter. But whereas there we were putting together a general description of three faith-situations, here we are talking about one of the direct consequences of being with Jesus.

The appropriateness of this feature, it seems to me, does not lie in the fact that Jesus himself often journeyed through the various towns and villages of Galilee. Nor does it stem from the fact that the Christian's basic way is the way of the cross, although Jesus' own life-journey led finally to Jerusalem and to his death. The sense of journeying arises, I suspect, because the disciple is growing in God, ascending into the holy mystery of God, moving closer to the divine presence. To know God in Jesus is to identify with the gospel narratives depicting the disciples "on the way" with Jesus. We imagine ourselves moving through life with Jesus who sometimes walks alongside of us and sometimes ahead of us. But while the story of Jesus' journeying through various towns and villages is represented geographically, our experience of moving with him is a journey of soul. In fact, it is actually the journey of God moving through our lives continually making and remaking our souls, that is, our inner selves. Sometimes it feels as if we are doing the journeying, but in reality God is the one who is moving, through us, and that movement is what we feel.

The one who follows Jesus is drawn into a movement of grace, into growing steadily in wisdom, discernment, fidelity, patience and familiarity with God. A person cannot be Jesus' follower without experiencing his or her mind and heart advancing in spiritual insight, inner freedom and love for the people of God. And the disciple never crosses the same spiritual terrain twice.

9.   For the disciple, being with Jesus also includes the *experi-ence of being taught*. Very noticeably in the Gospel of Mark, but in the other gospels too, Jesus is the teacher and the disciples are learners. In one episode aboard the boat, with a furious squall raging around them, they arouse him from sleep, panic-stricken: *"Teacher,* don't you care if we drown?" (Mk 4:38) That is the kind of question the followers of Jesus are likely to keep on asking whenever, as a result of being with him, they appear to be on the brink of disaster. And that is precisely the occasion when Jesus, the teacher, instructs his disciples to understand why no situation in their lives—if they are with him—is quite the way it initially seems.

In another scene, after pointing out the hypocrisy of the Pharisees and the teachers of the Law, Jesus warned them, "Nor are you to be called 'teacher,' for you have one teacher, the Christ" (Mt 23:10). To live our entire lives as people who are still being taught, still having our ignorance uncovered, still being given simple lessons about the love of God and the meaning of the kingdom, demands patience and considerable spiritual stamina. It may be reassuring to remember that even the first disciples never quite mastered the lessons of the kingdom. "Do you still not see or understand? Are your hearts hardened? Do you have eyes but fail to see, and ears but fail to hear? And don't you remember? . . . Do you still not understand? . . . Are you so dull?" (Mk 8:17-18,21; 7:18)

These episodes are reported—for our benefit, not for the sake of the first disciples!—during Jesus' public ministry. After he was taken from them, the disciples still had to depend upon the Spirit of Jesus to keep teaching them, guiding them, helping them to discern how best to fulfill his mission. "All this I have spoken while still with you," Jesus said. "But the Counselor, the Holy Spirit, whom the Father will send in my name, will teach you all things and will remind you of everything I have said to you" (Jn 14:25-26). Even after his resurrection, Jesus remains present among his followers, encouraging them, correcting their mistaken apprehensions about the nature of his ministry, and reassuring them of his unfailing love. Is this not the abiding consolation of the Emmaus story? To be with God in Christ is to find ourselves identifying with the stories of Jesus' first followers. The experience of being taught is simply another way of describing the experience of being created and redeemed, of growing in freedom and of being grasped by God's love.

10. A tenth aspect of the religious experience of Jesus' disciples is the *tension and struggle* they encounter as a result of their efforts to remain his faithful followers. The real religious problems for the disciples began *after* they came to know Jesus. If Jesus had not told them to walk the extra mile, to turn the other cheek, to lend without expecting repayment, never to harbor the lustful thought, to forgive seventy times seven times, to serve one another as they would serve Jesus himself, not to put their trust in worldly riches or accomplishments or their careers, to love their enemies, and so forth, then they certainly would never have felt their minds and hearts stretched so far and sometimes so painfully.

So too for us. Are we better off or worse off for coming to know Jesus? Was the rich young man of Mark 10 better off or worse off for having met Jesus? And what about the Pharisees, or the Samaritan woman of John 4, or Judas, or Peter, or Paul, or Pilate, or anyone else? Were they better off or worse off for having encountered Jesus? Some walked away from him, some faced inner struggles they had never dreamt of before, some would lose their lives, some would betray him. Considering the tension we often experience precisely because now we know that God expects nothing less than that we be perfect, many of us might be tempted to confess that in many ways our condition is far more precarious than before we came into contact with Jesus.

Paul's anguish in Romans 7 now becomes intelligible, doesn't it? To paraphrase his text, perhaps we could ask: Is the gospel sin? Is the gospel our stumbling block? By no means! But in order that we should see the dimensions of sinfulness and just how far from perfect freedom and full humanity we are, God has given us the gospel. Indeed, God has given us Christ so that we can discern precisely what coming to full stature as God's children demands. If we had not met Jesus, we would not be struggling over our resis-

tance toward prayer, our slowness to forgive. We would not be
striving to serve one another patiently, to do justice, to keep pure
minds and hearts, to live simply, and to love inclusively. Such
tension seems to be an unavoidable consequence of being with
Jesus, and if we feel this tension, then there is cause for thanking
God. This sort of tension is creative; it is a sign of the Spirit's
presence in our minds and hearts. To know God in Christ is to be
pulled into the tension and struggle of discipleship.[6]

11.   A strong *desire to pray* is yet another feature of being a
disciple. The disciples had observed Jesus praying on many different
occasions and in a variety of places. To be with God, as Jesus
obviously was, seemed to express itself naturally in frequent and
sometimes intense prayer. Jesus prayed the usual blessings at meal-
times. He prayed during synagogue worship, in the Temple, and
presumably at other prescribed times. Frequently he spent a whole
night in prayer or left his home early in the morning before others
were awake in order to pray in a secluded place.

This fidelity to prayer—the example of someone who seriously
wanted and needed to pray—powerfully attracted the disciples.
They not only remembered the many instances of Jesus at prayer as
they formed the traditions and stories about Jesus, but they also
wanted to be taught how to pray, intently and frequently, in all
circumstances. In being with Jesus they discovered themselves ever
more eager to be in the presence of God. Their desire to pray and
their awareness of their need to pray seem to be important aspects
of their experience as followers of Jesus. Why? Because Jesus prayed.
Jesus lived in the presence of God. But also, perhaps, because Jesus
uncovered for them their intuition that it is right and proper for
men and women to know God intimately. We want to know God.
We believe that some people actually do know God; therefore, it
should be possible for us to know God also. But often we feel so
inadequate and unholy. What makes us think that we have something to say to God, or that God would be interested in our
humble efforts to pray? Maybe we know how to do little more than
cry out with the first disciples, "Teacher, don't you care if we
drown?"

Being with Jesus, however, moves us beyond such feelings of unworthiness. Being with him, we are willing to learn how to pray. We want to be taught. For how can one be a disciple of Jesus and not know what it means to be familiar with God? Yet to know God in Christ is not only to want to pray, it is to want to pray with Jesus. To know God in Christ is to want to pray the way Jesus prayed and to experience the One whom he called Father.

12.   A final feature of the disciples' religious experience was their *identifying with Jesus in his dying and rising*. While this identifying with Jesus is most clearly evident in the letters of St. Paul, his experience must to some degree have been typical of many other followers. "If anyone would come after me," Jesus said, "he must deny himself and take up his cross daily and follow me" (Lk 9:23). For Paul, this feature appears in his declaration "I have been crucified with Christ" (Gal 2:20), which is to say, he is *still being crucified* in his daily following of Jesus. What he once counted as important now strikes him as worthless, compared to his life's new objective of gaining Christ, of being with Jesus. Weakness becomes strength, for God works through our human powerlessness and inadequacy just as God worked through the suffering and death of Jesus, and raised him from the dead.

But the victory was not simply Jesus' release from the grave. The power of God is manifested in the fact that the risen Jesus continued to work among his disciples. He continued to arouse in men and women the deepest of human and religious desires; he continued to be the source of forgiveness. The risen Jesus had become present to his followers in a totally new way. He encouraged them as they undertook the mission he had given them and, as the source of the new life they now shared, Jesus enabled them to form a new kind of human community. This is where the divine power was manifested. The disciples realized that as they lived the gospel and bore witness to Jesus, they had not been defeated. Theirs was not a gloomy following which knew that in the end what awaited the companions of Jesus was humiliation and rejection. No, they would never have followed Jesus and remained faithful to him after his death unless the way they were now walking confirmed itself with certain signs. And their way was confirmed. They discovered freedom, joy, community, a sense of mission, and the presence of the God whom Jesus knew as Father. Contrary to their reaction on the night of Jesus' betrayal, they were honored when the things which happened to Jesus also happened to them. In fact, Luke tells us, the disciples rejoiced "because they had been counted worthy of suffering disgrace for the Name" (Acts 5:41).

Death and resurrection form the basic rhythm of Christian existence. Identifying with Jesus in his dying and rising refers to the pattern of living which is defined by companionship with Jesus in his suffering and which, at the same time, hopes for—and often tastes—the new life into which God raised Jesus. Suffering is generally unavoidable in human life, but there is a difference between suffering with Jesus and suffering apart from him. There is a difference between making our life journey with Jesus and apart from him. There is a difference in approaching God in prayer with Jesus and without him. Loneliness endured with Jesus, or poverty, or sickness, or misunderstanding, or rejection, or the process of diminishment and death, is different when we are with Jesus and when we pass through life without him. In other words, to be drawn into the mystery of Jesus' dying means that we take up the cross and follow him. Crosses are inevitably part of life, but not every cross is that of Jesus. And so we learn how to be with him and to interpret our suffering and our humanity through the eyes of his faith. To the degree that we are with Jesus, the way we carry our humanity will be correspondingly affected, perhaps even transformed. Why? Because in dying for us, Jesus lifts our humanness to a new possibility. God loves us unconditionally. Our believing that this is the profound truth about human beings enables us to accept our own humanity and offer it to God so that God might work through it and fashion us into the divine image and likeness.

Yet dying is not the whole story; there is also a rising. Without resurrection, the suffering, limitations and sinfulness we must endure would burden us unremittingly. This would make us defeated people, unable to give any reasons for the hope which we have.

Without resurrection where would we find the confidence to face the future and to believe that God has championed the side of the peacemakers, the poor in spirit, the ones who hunger and thirst for justice, the merciful, the pure in heart?

God does offer some small signs along the way to assure us that our faith is not groundless. Again, we have to learn to view life with the eye of faith. There is indeed a victory over sin which we occasionally experience. There is the conviction that we would not have been able to repent and change our self-centering behavior without God's assistance. Likewise, there is the conviction born of faith that, having been dragged through an especially painful episode, God has blessed our struggle and graced the way to resolution, reconciliation, or perhaps to an acceptance of a situation which we cannot change. Life is not without moments of surprise, of wonder, of giftedness, or of unlooked-for peace. People can astonish us by their patience, or by their contrition, or by a sudden display of kindness. By the curious logic of grace, God can bring order out of chaos, honor out of disgrace, holiness out of human weakness, for frequently God grants us what we really want even though it may not correspond to what we had asked for. To experience anything in life with Jesus means that everything we undergo, every step of our passing through this world, every aspect of our living—whatever we think, dream, imagine, love, choose, repent, surrender, endure, or celebrate—is laced with hope in the holy mystery of God which daily calls us into existence. To rise with Jesus is to live from moment to moment as if we had just discovered his empty tomb. This is something which the disciple of Jesus continues to experience.

To be drawn into the mystery of Jesus' resurrection is to face life with the sureness which declares that no good work, no struggle in the cause of peace and justice, no effort at reconciliation and forgiveness, no desire to grow in compassion, no energy expended in the service of those God has given us to serve and to love, is useless, romanticized or worth only half-hearted measures. For every good work is rooted ultimately in the holy mystery which is patiently creating and redeeming the human race.

There are surely other facets of the religious experience of Jesus'
disciples which could be garnered from a close reading of the New
Testament. Each of the gospel stories recounts at least to some
degree how the first disciples experienced Jesus: what they did with
him, how they reacted to his teaching and example, what impressed
itself upon their memories, and so forth. But the gospels, as
accounts written by Christians who appeared on the scene after the
actual life of Jesus, also tell us something about the experience of
the second and third generation disciples. They too were experiencing the risen Lord, and this undoubtedly shaped the way they
handed on the stories about Jesus. Certainly in John, and frequently in the synoptic gospels as well, the reader suspects that the
Jesus who is speaking and acting is now the Lord, the one definitively with God, the new Law, the Savior.

Recall some of the ways in which Jesus is remembered as calling
people out of hiding. He draws out the woman at the well, perhaps
as she tried to conceal her shameful past from him. He draws Levi
from behind the tax collector's role and the tax collector's booth.
Jesus draws Peter out of his embarrassment, and keeps him from
covering himself in his shame and humiliation by eliciting from his
lips the true depth of his love. In one way or another, each time
Jesus forgave people he was calling men and women who were
hiding from God into the refreshing openness which belongs to
God's sons and daughters. They found God to be someone who
loved them as much as God loved Adam, or Abraham, or Isaiah, or
David; God's face was not one from which they had to flee. And,
of course, Jesus continues to do this among us.

The Jesus whom the disciples experienced enabled them to lay
aside all things for his sake. He was the one who joined them in
unexpected ways, as when he walked toward them at night across
the water, or when he accompanied two others as they made their
way to Emmaus. Recall the kinds of occasions when Jesus was with
them: during the storm on the lake, while they ate, in their
confrontations with political and religious authorities, when they
worshipped, in their homes. There are any number of situations
recorded in the gospels where the disciples are at the center and
Jesus is somehow drawn into their lives, into the contexts of their

living. The disciples are asked whether their teacher pays the temple tax, and Jesus is drawn into their predicament. The disciples are reminded, while walking through the grain fields on a Sabbath, that it is not lawful to be plucking grain (Lk 6:1ff.) The disciples are in a boat when the squall descends upon the lake, and Jesus is asleep at the edge of the scene.

More often we find situations in which Jesus is at the center and the disciples are with Jesus. They are drawn into the contexts of his living. During his public ministry they are with him when he feeds the crowds, or heals the sick, or forgives sinners, or is invited to a rich person's home for dinner. They are pulled into the circumstances of his life at the Last Supper, in his anguished prayer at Gethsemane, during his travels throughout Galilee and elsewhere, or when he needed to pray. Luke tells us, "Once when Jesus was praying in private and *his disciples were with him* . . ." (9:18). Even when Jesus is alone, his disciples are with him! And they will always be with him, even when in their fear they abandon him. The disciples experience Jesus as the one who overturns venerable traditions, who speaks and acts with authority, who gives prophetic witness to the values and concerns of God. They experience his faith, for the demons scramble at his word, the lame walk at his word, lepers are cleansed at his word, bread multiplies at his word. Jesus worked such signs not by virtue of some magical power, but through the power of his own faith that God would listen to his requests, even were he to ask the Father to move a mountain!

In short, the way the gospel stories are composed leads us to conclude that the disciples experienced Jesus coming into the situations of their lives, and they also found themselves drawn into situations within his life. This did not happen only during his ministry, while he lived among them. After Jesus' death the new site of Jesus' ministry is the church. As the church continues the mission of Jesus, the disciples of Jesus today still find themselves being drawn into the various contexts of his life. Where would we expect to find Jesus in today's world? The answer to that gives us the present context of his ministry, and the situation in which God's revealing action among us takes place. Jesus can transform the life-situation of his disciple so that he or she sees and judges things through the prism of the gospel. Everything is different if Jesus is in the scene. He enters the disciple's home, crises, work, fantasies and fears, or relationships, and becomes present there. But Jesus can also pull the disciple into situations where he or she is with him in his work, in his crises, in his serving and healing, in his prayer, in his prophetically witnessing to God's justice and mercy, in his suffering and betrayal, in his abandonment and death. The basic feature of the religious experience of Jesus' disciple is that he or she will always consciously and gratefully be living in his company.

The Changing Sense of Sin and Forgiveness in the Disciple's Life

One aspect of the Christian's growth in holiness which does not ordinarily make its way into the church's preaching and teaching is the changing sense of sinfulness which we may experience during the course of our lives. Yet this changing sense of sin also pertains to the religious experience of Jesus' disciples. The painful difference, at least in the way I imagine various gospel scenes, between the denial of Peter and the betrayal of Judas is that Peter was closer to Jesus than Judas was. The difference between Simon, the Pharisee who invited Jesus to dinner, and the sinful woman who wept at Jesus' feet while he sat at table is, as Jesus remarked, that "he loves little who has been forgiven little" (Lk 7:47). Which means, he loves little who does not realize how much forgiveness he truly needs. We have to surmise that the longer the disciples lived as companions of Jesus, the more sensitive they became to the ways in which hardness of heart could express itself. How foolish they must have felt when they recalled, in the weeks and months after the night they abandoned Jesus, that they had shortly before been arguing among themselves about who was closest to Jesus and thereby deserved the highest place in the kingdom of heaven!

In "Reflections on the Problem of the Gradual Ascent to Christian Perfection" Karl Rahner pointed out that our moral acts can be accompanied by greater or lesser degrees of intensity. As we grow in grace, presumably we bring deeper love, insight and freedom to whatever we do.[7] People certainly do make progress in the way of virtue (as long as they don't get caught in constantly trying to assess how much progress they have actually made). But it is not always easy to tell whether we are making a gradual ascent or whether we have stalled along the way. I would like to develop Rahner's idea by examining how our experience of sin and forgiveness might be affected as our relationship with Jesus becomes more mature.

It generally happens that the friends of God, the ones who have exemplified fidelity to the gospel and to Jesus, are more distressed by personal sin than those who are afraid of God. I don't mean to suggest that the friends of God begin discovering sins all over the place. Nor does their distress result from a frustrated desire to be perfect, as if the recurrence of sin in their lives were simply a matter of personal disappointment over moral failure. Rather, the sinfulness of the friends of God can feel all the more burdensome precisely because they have grown familiar with the Lord. They realize more clearly than the rest of us what exactly sin is. In a strange sort of religious irony, it may be that only the friends of God know what they are doing when they sin. The rest of us can be excused and forgiven because we do not know, at least not very well, what we are doing to ourselves. Hans Urs von Balthasar writes:

> The disobedience of one who loves to even the least wishes of love is much more serious than that of one who is far from love, who hardly suspects the existence of love or of the laws of love. Both the internal and external actions of one who loves are weighed in a different balance; such a one calls in vain upon the larger distinctions that are valid for others. A wish that God whispers in his ear because there is a possibility that it may be heard, but which he rejects, can wound God's eternal love more deeply than the transgression of a major commandment by one who is as yet unaware of the rules that govern the etiquette of love.[8]

The reaction of the friends of God to their wrongdoing is not simply a bit of spiritual play-acting. They are not merely exaggerating ordinary faults and failures. Their reaction to personal sin is not a matter of religiously edifying pretense staged for God's benefit. Rather, the closer they come to God, the more aware they become of what God really desires. The more they are drawn into the mystery of God's radically inexplicable love for us, then the more troubled they are by their own sinfulness. This feeling arises, not out of disappointment over a lapse in spiritual growth, as if they had broken, say, a New Year's resolution, but out of concern for the glory and love of God. For the friends of God, sin is what keeps them from the One who has expressed nothing but love toward human beings. Sin shows itself as ingratitude, as heady independence, as the forgetfulness of divine love. Even more, sin shows itself as distance or separation, as the thing which keeps friends of God from being fully united to the source of their life.

Still, God's judgment about sin and human judgment about sin are two different things. From a divine viewpoint—if I can presume to talk this way—sin is the creature's refusal to be fully human and fully free. It is a rejection of the Creator's love which daily calls us into existence. We ask God for so many things, and yet only one thing really matters. Only one thing is of real concern to God, namely, that we come to our full stature as men and women, finally fashioned into the divine image and likeness. The story of a person's sinfulness has to be read with an eye to God's ongoing, lifelong creating of us. There are depths to our freedom and regions of our consciousness of which we may be only dimly aware. In fact, we might not be at all conscious of the limitations upon our freedom or the nature of our deeper motives and promptings. Every human being remains a mystery to himself or herself, no matter how self-actualized and mature the individual might appear in his or her own eyes, or to the rest of us. The reason is that intertwined with human freedom is the steady and generally imperceptible action of God's grace. Our deepest drives do not necessarily coincide with our conscious longings, but the grace of God works both on our consciousness and beneath it. It leavens the hundreds of small actions, decisions, thoughts and daydreams of daily life, conspiring with the source of all good desires in us—our own spirit—to lead us toward a way of acting and thinking which is ever more patient, more compassionate and more attuned to the presence of God.

What God sees, therefore, is the steady transformation of the human being under the attraction of grace; we can never completely follow this. God beholds our individual actions against the broader horizon of our lives: who and what we are, what we have become, who and what we shall one day be. This is a perspective we obviously cannot share. Yet it is important to recall that in the matter of human sinning, what God sees and how God judges will be quite different from the way we perceive our own sinfulness or the sins committed by those around us.

The human standpoint for judging personal sinfulness is neither detached nor privileged. We simply do not possess enough information about ourselves or about others to give a balanced, realistic picture of how we stand before God. But the experience of being a sinner is something else. We do experience ourselves as sinful people who need the healing power of God's love. We know that we want to be saved and redeemed from the hold that sin—the life-denying force at work in our lives—has upon us. We do experience how unfinished our discipleship is, and we can easily recognize ourselves in Jesus' words to the disciples along the Emmaus road: "How foolish you are, and how slow of heart to believe all that the prophets have spoken!" (Lk 24:25)

An Ignatian Model

The classical ascetical tradition distinguished three stages in an individual's ascent to spiritual perfection: purgation, illumination and contemplative union. As a Jesuit, I am more comfortable with the model of Christian discipleship which emerges from St. Ignatius Loyola's *Spiritual Exercises*. The Ignatian model follows the pattern of the gospels: repentance, following, suffering and death, resurrection. The individual is called to repentance, invited to be a disciple of Jesus, drawn to be a companion of Jesus in his suffering and death, and finally, missioned by Jesus to be his witness before the world. These stages of discipleship can serve as a lens or a framework for viewing Christian experience.

The model is a dynamic one. This means that those who have

just experienced the grace of being invited to discipleship, for example, will view their sinfulness differently from—not, mind you, better than—someone who is hearing for the first time Jesus' call for change of heart. Those who imagine themselves standing with the beloved disciple at the foot of the cross will view their sinfulness differently from someone imaginatively walking among the disciples when they begin arguing about who is the greatest. And the model applies to other things besides personal sinfulness. Our sense of mission, our comprehension of who Jesus is, our sense of being church, our attitude toward the world—all of these things also change and develop if in fact we are trying to follow and be faithful to Jesus.

Corresponding to the first stage of discipleship is the experience of being a loved sinner. The awareness of sin during this moment of discipleship might consist of those grave disorders or occasions in which we resist or deny our creaturehood. It certainly includes individual actions which we realize are wrong, but our sense of their wrongness is proportioned to how bluntly we see the many ways in which God has been so good to us. Through the prayer of this stage our minds and hearts have become attuned to their need to praise and thank God, and the more we want to praise God, the more struck and embarrassed we are about how deaf and blind we have been to the love which brought us into being. Here sin shows its most destructive aspect through its capacity to keep us from believing that we have been loved. The disciple experiences divine forgiveness while contemplating the crucified Jesus and realizing that Jesus died out of love for us. From the cross divine love chases our sins out of hiding. Even at our worst God in Christ is there to love us, to draw us, to heal and create us.

In the second stage we have to endure our failures in discipleship. We know that Jesus called us to be his followers, and we have accepted that call eagerly and gratefully. Yet now we feel the struggle between the old not fully converted self and the new way of the gospel. Gospel values become increasingly important, but there remains a considerable amount of misunderstanding as to what Jesus stands for. Perhaps we latch onto an excessively literalist reading of the gospel texts, or a rigorous approach to the practice of discipleship. Maybe like John the Baptist we yield to some disillusionment because Jesus is too lenient, because he doesn't fast and abstain from strong drink like a professional prophet, or because he keeps bad company and allows himself to be touched by the wrong kind of people. Maybe we are uncomfortable about the fact that even he could be tempted, or that he was so demanding about forgiveness. There is much to learn.

The disciple has zeal but still needs to be taught about the Spirit's way. Perhaps like some of the figures in the gospels, we find ourselves anxious and worried about the wrong things, or too easily overcome by fear, or falling asleep in times of prayer. Ordinary human faults, which previously merely seemed ordinary, now appear as disloyalty to Jesus. We sometimes feel like a child in school. Our mistakes often feel so foolish, so stupid. At other times, we undergo that tension of discipleship and ask, Are we better off or worse off for having come to know Jesus? Maybe here forgiveness is experienced in terms of the Jesus who does not go away. Exasperated by how slowly his disciples comprehended his message and example, and by the dullness of their hearts to the values of God's kingdom, Jesus might have dismissed them and searched for other followers who would prove more reliable. But Jesus stayed with them; he did not send them away. The experience of Jesus' remaining despite the weakness of their efforts and their proneness to forgetting or ignoring his teaching is itself an experience of acceptance and forgiveness.

The third stage is that of being with the suffering Jesus as friend and companion. Here we are gradually yet forcefully drawn into solidarity with the suffering of Jesus in his brothers and sisters. Perhaps in this stage the sense of sin entails not being fully aware of and responsive to the demands of justice, being unavailable to others, failures in compassion, and a narrowly nationalistic way of looking at the world and its problems. The longer we spend in Jesus' company and the more refined our religious sensibilities become, the more aware we are of how much has yet to be redeemed. We begin to grasp that much of our sinfulness is locked within us and remains impervious to the searching light of awareness unless God helps us. We may not be committing gravely evil actions, but now those actions are all the more humiliating and seem all the more serious precisely because we have drawn so close to Jesus. Think of Peter when the rooster crowed.

Forgiveness at this stage of discipleship might show itself as our being allowed to share Jesus' experience of humiliation and suffering. Jesus accepts us into his company. Not only does he refuse to dismiss us as recalcitrant disciples, Jesus really wants us to be with him where he is: to feel *his* anguish, to share *his* rejection and humiliation, to experience *his* feelings of abandonment and thirst. How could Jesus more effectively tell us of his forgiving love than by inviting us to stay with him along the way of the cross? Forgiveness might sound like a curious way to describe this sort of religious experience, but I believe that is what it is. To be forgiven is to be accepted, and in this stage the Father accepts the disciples of Jesus to be with him wherever in the world he suffers hunger, or thirst, or imprisonment, or rejection, or betrayal, or torture, or death.

The disciple in the fourth stage of the Ignatian model has been given the grace of finding God in all things. This is an Easter grace. The risen Jesus went ahead of his disciples into Galilee. But the risen Jesus is always going ahead of his disciples, and so Galilee becomes a symbol of every place in the world, for there is no place where we cannot discover the risen Lord if indeed we are eagerly looking for him. In fact Easter Christians gradually discern a new depth in every aspect of life—in every person, in every place, in every circumstance and event—because the Spirit of the risen Jesus helps us to see everything from the perspective of God's love for the world.

The sinfulness which we might now experience is the failure to pray with sufficient energy and regularity. One misses clues for where Jesus is, or what he is doing in the world, just as the first disciples stood before the empty tomb uncomprehendingly, or walked away from Jerusalem with downcast faces, or locked themselves behind closed doors out of fear, or in their bewilderment tried to resume the routines they followed before Jesus had entered their lives. Sinfulness here could also translate into not searching aggressively for signs of Jesus' presence in everyday life and in the world. It is a retreat into a pattern of living which ventures little and risks nothing for the sake of the gospel: we are afraid to trust that Jesus really is there ahead of us. Or the sense of sin might manifest itself as the failure to live as an Easter Christian, that is, to live in such a way that our life only makes sense because Jesus has been raised from the dead. To some degree, the Easter Christian should always be countercultural.

The risen Jesus keeps greeting his disciples with "Peace!" He rebuilds their fallen hopes; he recalls them into communion with each other and with himself. The risen Jesus empowers his disciples with the Spirit of freedom. No longer are they imprisoned behind locked doors, afraid that what happened to Jesus might happen to them. No longer are they concerned about their possessions, or about who will hold the higher place in heaven, or about upsetting those in positions of authority. They don't have to act deferentially to those who are wealthy, or politically powerful, or well-placed in the Sanhedrin. They have discovered a new experience of freedom, the freedom that comes from knowing Jesus and from the conviction that Jesus has sent them into the world as his witnesses. Forgiveness here is related to the sense of mission, to the experience of being chosen by God and anointed with the Spirit of Jesus. In the fourth stage the grace of forgiveness comes as we experience ourselves being set free for a life-mission, increasingly able to find peace—and sometimes even joy—in things from which we once ran in fear. Forgiveness is the experience of being loved, chosen, and sent. Forgiveness is the freedom which comes from being with Jesus wherever he wants to be.

My reason for drawing out this model is simple. It helps to illuminate the gradual ascent to Christian perfection. There is real religious development, real ascent into the holy mystery of God. But it is often accompanied by a humbling sort of peace. The saints who confessed themselves to be great sinners were not joking or pretending a false modesty, and we should not dismiss their claims as overdrawn. They spoke out of profound self-knowledge, for they realized better than the rest of us that they were living in the presence of God. They also knew better the meaning of divine mercy, and thus they felt overwhelmed by goodness and enormously grateful. We don't have to go looking for sin. It seems to catch up with us the moment we accept God's invitation to follow Jesus.

When we look at ourselves, what do we see? Do we see that pride which doesn't want to show itself, which hides behind a defensive confidence and says, "I am a sincere, honest person trying my best to do what God expects of me?" Do we see the self-centeredness which often runs alongside what we thought were our most selfless gestures? Do we see that in countless instances we have been living as if we don't really need God, although we have been telling God how much we depend upon God's help? Has our declared reliance upon God often prevented us from feeling estranged from true holiness? Have we felt close to God, yet at the same time wondered why our experience of God has been so undramatic, so lacking in intensity?

Have we declared ourselves poor, perhaps even attempting to live simply and frugally, before we have tasted our inner poverty, the failure of good intentions, the steady erosion of faith by losing ourselves in good works and believing that we have merited God's special affection? Have we said yes to God, promising our loyalty and love, only to be looking for ways to break that promise without appearing in God's eyes to have sinned? Have we excused ourselves by telling ourselves that we are only human, that no one can realistically keep lifelong promises without knowing what the future will bring? Have we taught our children, by our example if not by our words, that a person can serve God and something else? And after all this, do we dare to take refuge by apologizing to God that we are imperfect creatures who cannot be expected always to do what is right? I think, honestly, we may have to answer yes to questions such as these. By the time sinfulness dawns upon us in this way, however, we shall have already moved a considerable distance along the way of discipleship. If this catches the tone of our sinfulness then we should take heart. The grace of God has already been drawing us out of hiding.

FOOTNOTES

1. For a detailed comment on the Lord's Prayer in Luke, see Joseph A. Fitzmyer, *The Gospel According to Luke X—XXIV* (New York: Doubleday & Co., 1985), pp. 896-901.

   Also, see the entry under "Lord's Prayer" in *The Interpreter's Dictionary of the Bible*, vol. 3 (Nashville: Abingdon Press, 1962).

2. James D. G. Dunn, *Jesus and the Spirit* (Philadelphia: Westminster Press, 1975), p. 342.

3. On the meaning of the personal pronouns see Raymond E. Brown, *The Epistles of John* (New York: Doubleday & Co., 1982), pp. 462-466.

4. Vatican II, *Pastoral Constitution on the Church in the Modern World*, no. 41.

5. The full implications of this aspect of discipleship would take many pages to unfold. A good book on understanding and living out Jesus' call to become poor today is John Kavanagh's *Following Christ in a Consumer Society* (Maryknoll, N.Y.: Orbis Books, 1981).

6. Dunn, op. cit. pp. 308-318.

7. Karl Rahner, *Theological Investigations*, vol. 3: *The Theology of the Spiritual Life*, trans. Karl-H. and Boniface Kruger (New York: Crossroad Publishing Co., 1982), pp. 3-23.

8. Hans Urs von Balthasar, *The Christian State of Life*, trans. Mary Frances McCarthy (San Francisco: Ignatius Press, 1983), p. 38.

CHAPTER 4

The Life of the Believer as Revelation of the Mystery of God

Thus it is evident to everyone that all the faithful of Christ of whatever rank or status are called to the fullness of the Christian life and to the perfection of charity.

The Church, to which all are called in Christ Jesus, and in which we acquire sanctity through the grace of God, will attain her full perfection only in the glory of heaven.
—Vatican II, *Dogmatic Constitution on the Church*

In his biography about Thomas Merton, Michael Mott made a passing reference to a conversation which Merton had with the Dalai Lama:

The Dalai Lama asked a number of questions about Western monasticism and showed a particular interest in vows, wondering if the vow was intended to be the beginning or the end of a monk's spiritual journey, a subject that was certainly close to Merton and to Merton's own sense of spiritual journey. [1]

I have often thought about the same question. In the broader context of Christian life, and not simply in the case of monastic or religious life, I believe we can ask whether the same question applies to every follower of Christ. Do the promises we make at baptism, and which we implicitly renew each time we receive the eucharistic bread and share the cup of communion with Christ, mark what we expect of ourselves as we start or resume our journey of discipleship, or do they point to what we hope to become only after a lifetime of striving to be faithful companions of Jesus? To put the matter a little differently, do the promises signal an "already" or a "not yet," something we have achieved or something we hope to accomplish by the end of our lives?

The issue which the Dalai Lama voiced is hardly a matter of words. The baptismal promises are, to use a technical term, eschatological; that is, they anticipate what we hope we shall become as a result of years of being faithful and loyal to Jesus. The promises steady our resolve. They direct our religious awareness, our conscious efforts to develop our freedom and not to waste our lives with aimless choices and thoughtless behavior. Like the vows pronounced at marriage, or the vows taken by men and women entering religious communities, but even more radically, the baptismal promises commit us to an evangelical way of life. They announce before the church and the world what kind of people we want to become. Daily we try to live those promises as best we can, but we do not pretend to have completely realized in our living what the promises contain. We do not pretend to have incarnated the gospel from the outset of our lives as disciples any more than married couples claim to have already become the living sign of faithfulness, of mutually sanctifying affection, of a living oneness in mind and heart when they stand before the believing community, state their intentions and exchange their vows. The baptismal promises declare what we intend: that we are sinful people who desire to follow Jesus and who know that we cannot hope to remain with him unless he pledges to be with us. As Origen, the great biblical scholar of the third century, wrote, "Faith in its full sense is accepting with one's whole soul what is professed at baptism."[2]

We would be unable to keep our promises if we had only our own strength to depend upon. Without the believing community to support us, without other men and women to sustain us by their example, by their encouragement and advice, by their prayers to God on our behalf, by their patient acceptance of our sinfulness, we would not be able to stay faithful to Jesus. We would lose heart if we did not have a sense of God's providential care. We might abandon the practice of our religion altogether unless we were strongly convinced that God had taken the initiative in leading us into the community of believers where we could learn about Jesus. How else could we dare to renew the baptismal promises sincerely, those phrases which encapsulate our belief about what human beings are supposed to become, namely, men and women of God?

Between the promise and its fulfillment there lies a lifelong effort to be a believer in the fullest sense of the word. Along the way our lives can change direction any number of times, and often the direction our life takes is not totally planned. Some circumstances we do not foresee. We may be forced to abandon career goals in midstream. Because so many of the political, social and economic conditions of our time are beyond our personal control (not to mention our interpersonal relationships or our having to accept the personalities and freedom of others), it is no wonder that the dominant thread of our lives sometimes appears to have been imposed upon us. What we become, in other words, is not only a matter of what we choose to become. It is also a matter of being shaped by events, by the personalities and decisions of other people, as well as by factors in our own personalities of which we are unaware and about which there may be little we can do anyway.

The point of stating all this is to remind ourselves that we can find God in any number of circumstances, and that it is always possible for God to reach us, no matter how disordered the pattern of our living looks. A person might have married any one of a number of people, and his or her life in that event would unquestionably have been quite different. A person could have joined any of several religious communities; life would have been different with another set of companions, a different spiritual tradition, or another apostolic focus. Nevertheless, we still would have found God, and God would still call, teach and create us.

Reading Merton's biography brought home to me why there cannot be a science of the spiritual life. There can be a science only where it is possible to generalize, to move from the particular instance to the universal law. But Christian spirituality does not admit of many generalizations. It teaches some broad maxims, such as the responsibility to love God with all our heart, soul, mind and strength, and to love our neighbors as we love ourselves. It teaches about virtue, methods of prayer, the requirements of evangelical

living, and so forth. In short, Christian spirituality has built up a
fund of tested religious answers and directions for leading a holy
life.

But what humility means for one person may spell timidity, or
pride, for someone else. Obedience for one might become cowardice, even intellectual laziness, for another. What appears to be
charity might, upon discernment, prove itself to have been an
indiscreet or imprudent, even a harmful way of acting. Reticence to
correct another might be one person's way of keeping the Lord's
word about not judging our brother or sister, but it might also arise
from a fear of confrontation or from personal insecurity. What is
too much prayer for one person may be too little for another. What
poverty implies for one becomes affluence for somebody else. In the
process of testing and discerning—discerning where the Spirit of
God is leading our spirit—the heart of the matter is the individual's
experience of God. After listening carefully to the questions, the
advice and the wisdom of those who can help us to interpret our
experience, ultimately each of us must make a determination
personally about what our experience has been and where God
appears to be drawing us. In the practice of Christian spirituality,
therefore, we are nearly always dealing with the particular instance.

The Merton story raised a number of issues. His life in the
monastery resulted from a breakthrough experience, a religious
moment rich in consolation and strengthened with freshly won
fervor. But the conversion did not displace his native restlessness,
nor did it settle him so firmly in his commitment to monastic life
that he could not, at 50 years of age, fall in love with a hospital
nurse and contemplate marriage, or at least having her share his
hermitage! His journey may be a parable for the rest of us. His story
by no means need be typical of other religious people living behind
the walls of a monastic enclosure. Merton's faults do not give us
any permission to be casual about our own practice of discipleship.
Yet it is quite clear that grace does not transform our nature into
something it previously was not. We do not become totally different people as the immediate result of a religious conversion. Much
of the old man or the old woman remains, to haunt us, to provide

the material for our struggle to reach a more Christ-like way of being human, and to give glory to God.

The weaknesses which each of us carries are not necessarily always evil. As Paul wrote toward the end of his Second Letter to the Corinthians, if we must boast, let us boast about our weaknesses so that the power of God might be more clearly manifested in us. Merton's restlessness, which seemed at times to border on instability, also testifies to the persistent searching, self-examining and spiritual probing which accompany every believer's way to God. Perhaps the rest of us do not share Merton's penchant for keeping such remarkably candid journals. We may not share either his ability to notice the heart's many conflicting movements and desires or his alert reactions to situations and events. But we too have our feelings. We react to things, and we are tempted. How many times in the course of a day or a week, sometimes even in the space of an hour, do we change our minds, or do we imagine that people around us have deliberately set out to misinterpret what we have done? How many people do we imagine to be hostile to us? How many worst-case scenarios have we daydreamed which not only never came to pass, but which would never have even occurred to anyone but us? How many times have we moved from the spirit of prayer to the seamy attractions of lustful fantasies, or of having the upper hand over someone we don't like, or of finding excuses for avoiding what charity urges us to do?

How is it possible for a person like Merton, assuring himself that God understands his loneliness and his needs, to place portions of his sinfulness into brackets and to persuade himself that what would be wrong for others has somehow become right for him? After comparing Merton's account of his early days in the monastery from the pages of *The Seven Storey Mountain* with the later information from his letters and journals, how do we distinguish between loss of fervor and genuine, sobering religious growth? Or does Merton's life tell us that our approach to holiness, our slow ascent into the holy mystery of God, is *always* accompanied by doubt, ambiguity and the sinful tendencies we thought had been buried at the baptismal font, with our marriage vows or at the monastery door?

At first glance Merton seems an unlikely candidate for a model of Christian holiness in our time. Dorothy Day, who spent her life tirelessly working among New York's poor and unemployed, or Mother Teresa, who has commanded the world's attention in her service to the poor of Calcutta, or Archbishop Oscar Romero, the outspoken defender of human rights who was martyred while at the altar, might be worthier examples of Christian witness in the latter half of the 20th century. Yet although some might be reluctant to propose Merton as a model of Christian witness in our time, his life illustrates very well, I think, the irregular, complicated and uncertain ascent to God which increasingly characterizes the spiritual life of many men and women today. They do not doubt the integrity of the gospel, but they do believe that God is present in other world religions. And they wonder whether, at a time when many people have been drifting away from organized religion and appear neither to be aware of nor to care about the mystery of God in their lives, God will automatically dismiss such people from the rolls of the redeemed. They do not subscribe to sexual license, but they do complain about the rigidness of the church's traditional approach to sexuality. When they are alone with God, they start to crave the company of others; when they are around others at Mass, they begin hankering after privacy and solitary worship. The faith certainties with which they were raised no longer seem relevant to their present experience. They would not admit that those beliefs are untrue. They have simply arrived at the conclusion that many of the things they were taught about God and religion do not matter any more. They are not sure for which value, or set of values, or for which cause, they would put their lives on the line. Being uncertain about where they would make the ultimate sacrifice means that they have lost to some degree their sense of direction. They do not know where they, the church, their society, or the world might be heading.

Merton's uncertainty about the future of monastic life, his pessimism about the political and social problems of the '60s, his difficulties with religious authority in the monastery, his groping toward that peace, fulfillment, enlightenment and stability which kept eluding him, his need to be around people at the same time that he was trying to live in greater solitude as a hermit, his appreciation of music, poetry and art, his recurrent dissatisfaction over the kind of person he had apparently become, his strong need to win acceptance from others and to be reassured that he was worth loving—all these features belong to the portrait of a typically 20th-century person. Merton is a study in contrasts and tensions. Contrast, tension, complexity and doubt have become dominant colors in the picture of many believers today.

Let us turn to another story for a moment. With his retelling of the myth of Psyche and Eros in *Till We Have Faces*, C. S. Lewis put his finger on one of the perennial insights of Christian spirituality. Two sisters, one so ugly she passes through life with her face veiled and the other so beautiful that she is spirited away by a god, represent two sides of the self. The ugly sister, who becomes a wise and beloved queen, spends most of her life seeking the sister who was taken away from her. When she realizes that she must surrender all hope of ever having her beautiful sister back, she grows resentful of the god for depriving her of the one she loves. All her life she pursues the beauty which she cannot possess. Finally, in a dream, the queen is brought to a pool in which she sees not her own appearance, but the reflection of the sister she loved; the ugly woman has come to have a beautiful face. What she beholds is the reflection of an inward beauty. She is transformed as a result of her searching and the sorrow she endured; she realizes the misery that she has caused by wanting to possess what could not be hers. Through suffering, in other words, she becomes the beautiful sister for whom she had been searching so long.

Now, the point of Lewis' version of the story, at least as I interpret it, is this. The ugly self cannot possess the beautiful self because the beautiful self belongs to God; that is the insight we must sooner or later arrive at. There appear to be three facets to this insight. First, there is the ugly self which wants to be loved but is convinced that it is not worth loving. We are afraid to let others see this self; we fear that they might run away either laughing or terrified. Then there is the self we project, hoping that others will find it lovable. This self, however, is not the true self. In fact, it is not a self at all; it is only a mask. We use it to cover the face we believe to be ugly; we fear the wretched face that we have, or that we think we have, and so we spend our lives in hiding. Finally, there is the beautiful self we want to possess yet cannot, because that self belongs to God. This is the self we want to be, the self we shall be as a result of our journeying. It is also the self which God wants, the self which is made for God, the self which only God can possess. In the end there is something lovable about us after all, but what makes us desirable is God's desiring us. Whatever God loves is thereby lovable, and whatever is lovable is so because of God. God alone determines what is beautiful; God is the one who loves us, first and finally. In the end the desirable self is our only self, and that is the self which God always sees. This is a point about which John S. Dunne and Sebastian Moore have written eloquently.[3]

C. S. Lewis' story appeals to our imagination. He helps us to feel something we dimly perceive about ourselves. For we feel, at least sometimes, that we have spent a great portion of our lives searching for another, different self, the other half of who we are. We feel incomplete, and in our restlessness we reach out in many confused, generally misguided ways to seize that other self—that projected beauty—which keeps slipping from our grasp. That beauty, we sense, would finally make us whole and worth loving. There *may* be a connection between Merton's story and Lewis' recounting of the ancient myth. But there *is* a connection between each of these stories and the notion of revelation. Merton's story sheds light on the life of the believer as a revelation of the mystery of God, and the Lewis tale illustrates the view of revelation as our being uncovered and discovering a beauty inside ourselves which we would never have thought possible. However, there would be nothing beautiful to see apart from the desiring, the struggle, the sacrifice, the painful lessons, and the realization that the self we seek will never belong to us; it can only belong to God. All of which gives a different twist to "whoever loves his life will lose it." For to love our life in the proper sense, that is, to love the life which comes from God, means that we will have to yield that life back to God. And to lose our life because we have let God take possession of it, that is to find it.

It does not ease our restlessness to be reminded that the heart will always be unsettled until it rests in God, or that no place, no occupation, no relationship, no talent, no material possession can satisfy the heart's longing. Yet to say that God alone will satisfy us might induce some people to think that they must seek God in the way they look for and try to acquire anything else. Clearly that will not work. But why not? And why is it not sufficient just to have someone explain what is wrong with the way we have been looking for God?

The simplest way to answer this question is to say that God is a mystery and therefore unfathomable. We cannot lay hold of God, we cannot compel God to become present to us, and we cannot accelerate the development of our faith. But we already know this. How then ought we to look for God? If the divine mystery is beyond our comprehension, should we spend our time pursuing something other than contemplation? Would we be better advised to be engaged in Christian social action, service of our neighbor, or working on behalf of peace and justice?

The solution, I think, is this. We cannot dispense with action in coming to know God, since knowing God is not so much a theoretical as a practical concern. God is the one who acts, who creates, who is ever drawing human beings toward communion. For us, however, Jesus' example provides the key. His one desire was to do the Father's will. He sought solitude and he prayed, but Jesus was not a mystic who had withdrawn from the world. He did not make his home in the wilderness or in a monastic community. Jesus' place was among the towns and villages of Israel, in homes and synagogues, in the marketplaces where people gathered. If the life of Jesus reflects anything about the God who sent him, then surely we have every reason to conclude that God in Jesus was actively seeking out those who had lost their way, forgiving them, instructing, healing, creating. To know God is to be sent; it is to discover that our life has become mission. To know God in Jesus is to serve our neighbor.

Matthew 25 confirms the point that knowing God is an eminently practical concern. What do we "know" when we visit the imprisoned or comfort those who are sick? What do we "know" when we help the hungry to find food or the thirsty to find water? What do we "know" when we sit up patiently with a friend, a spouse or a child who is suffering a physical, emotional or religious crisis? What do we "know" when service to our families, our community or our neighbor means not being able to eat or sleep when we want to? What do we "know" when sharing with others means being unable to buy something we wanted for ourselves? What do we "know" when standing up for our convictions arouses misunderstanding and resentment among those closest to us, or when loyalty to Jesus' teaching makes others regard us as foolish, naive or impractical? In all these things we know the rightness of our action. We know that what we are doing is exactly the thing we should be doing, exactly what the moment demands of us. We know what it means to do what is right and good, without self-justifying reasons, without apology or excuse, without feelings of guilt or of being martyred, without any other motive except that we wish to do what is right. If that is what we truly want, then that is also what we truly love. What then are we loving when we do what is right, what Jesus calls us to? We are loving what is good, we are loving ourselves, and we are loving the holy mystery of God which has centered itself in the core of our souls.

What does a person know who, despite hardship, despite the sacrifice of his or her own future, security, even health, remains faithful to a promise? What does a person know who has acquired patience and compassion? What does a person know who faces life humbly and gratefully? What has a person learned whose inner strength comes not from having achieved worldly success, but from having suffered? Such a person knows that life can only be won by acknowledging it to be a gift, not by wresting it from the future. Such a person knows that the quality of life is measured in terms of giving, that the only religious way to respond to life is through acknowledgement (through *eucharistia*), no matter what happens to us. Such a person knows this not from going to school or reading it in a book. He or she knows this by going through life and experiencing the process of self-emptying. For the believer—and this is what makes such a person a believer in the first place—self-emptying does not spell loss and defeat. It spells recovery of soul and self.

Once again, if the life of Jesus informs us of anything here, surely it confirms the truth which Paul recorded: "He made himself nothing" (Phil 2:7). If Jesus is leading us to understand anything about God, certainly Jesus is saying that even God clings to nothing when the salvation of the human race is at stake.

If the Son of God empties himself and surrenders his life for our sake, then what on our side is so terribly important that we should not let go of it for the sake of one another? To know selflessness, therefore, is to know God. Not all suffering, not everything which men and women endure, is self-emptying. Suffering can be refused. I don't mean the avoidable discomfort which arises, for example, from not taking proper care of our health. I mean the suffering which arises from having our selfishness ground away by the unpleasant, trying and bitter moments of human life. When people consistently refuse to allow their self-centering fantasies, choices and activities to be burned away, then they will undergo life's diminishment unwillingly. There will be no self-emptying and, consequently, no knowledge of God. Purgatory is an inevitable aspect of the human journey; hell is not. But if we simply refuse the purging, then we invite the prospect of permanent self-enclosure. Ironically, those who pursue things only to satisfy themselves must endure the ultimate frustration of never being fulfilled. The things they aim for will never satisfy the human heart's hunger for life.

Action—doing—is absolutely essential for coming to know God. We have to do the God-like thing if we are to experience God. It often helps to have someone or some community assisting us in clarifying our actions and desires, and in evaluating our experience. Some people do the right thing—they lead upright, virtuous lives— without ever thinking of God. Recall those who wondered in that judgment scene from Matthew 25: "Lord, when did we see you hungry and feed you, or thirsty and give you something to drink? . . . When did we see you sick or in prison and go to visit you?" Human experience needs to be enriched by faith, by stories of God (like this one from Matthew), or by stories of men and women who have searched for God, if we are to experience the fullness of God's presence among us. How shall we locate God unless we have some idea of what we are looking for? How shall we interpret our experience religiously unless we are instructed about what God is like? Without the gospel—without the lesson in being human which Jesus himself exemplifies—we hold little chance of understanding the meaning of God's reign in the world. Unless they are schooled in the way of the gospel, Christians will be cheated of the consoling grace of living in the presence of Jesus.

I stress the importance of everyday things because human lives are, for the most part, made up of small events and ordinary joys, problems and concerns. Anyone who keeps searching for the big picture, the grand providential design which will tie all of life's loose ends together, will be sorely disappointed. Here a remark of John Dominic Crossan is appropriate. The familiar mustard seed parable Jesus used to describe the kingdom of God was not about a seed which grew into a towering cedar in whose branches eagles would nest, but about a tiny seed which grew into a shrub with ordinary birds—sparrows—pecking for food in its shade.[4] Not a flattering kingdom image, but true to life. And so also with us. There is probably no grand design which defines and establishes in concrete detail the meaning and value of our existence, certainly not a design which will show that the circumstances of our lives have been planned by God.

I am convinced that our lives unfold under God's providential concern, and I am equally convinced that we have to set our sights on the ordinary. The world we inhabit is small. Undertaking a spiritual quest for the ultimate meaning of our lives will not remedy the fundamental smallness of our world. Our happiness lies in picking up our humanity and discovering the meaningfulness of the things we are called upon to do each day. And what is that? Meaningfulness emerges from the sense of God's involvement in daily living. We are aware of meaningfulness to the extent that we experience ourselves as called by God, for if we are called, then we must be important. God, we have to believe, wants us. God knows us by name. God's hands shape and fashion us. We believe in God's call within the depths of our being. Knowing that God wants us and that we are desirable to God makes all the difference in the world. The ordinary becomes the extraordinary without plucking us from the small, everyday details of human living.

Why one person's life takes one direction while somebody else's follows a very different course is impossible to determine. Yes, considering people's family backgrounds, we can undoubtedly piece together the various influences which shaped them one way or another. But even then no one could infallibly predict the outcome since individuals from the same or similar backgrounds often pursue widely different paths. The basic issue is not to spend time fretting over whether God has a special need for us and confers some distinctive purpose upon our lives. All of us want to be special, but we can mistake being special for being called to do some great, heroic work. And who decides what makes a life's work great? For God, work is not what makes a person special or chosen. God, after all, can raise up children to Abraham from stones. That place is special where we find God, and we are already special because God has been looking for us. The sign of our having come close to God is not our profession, or our vocational choice, or our setting up shelters in Calcutta, or our being martyred. It is not whether we have had visions, or attained the heights of mysticism; it is not whether we have had great wealth to renounce or just a few trinkets. The sign of our having grown close to the mystery of God is whether we have allowed God to draw us out of our pretensions and our hiding, away from our unwillingness to have our affections purified, and into the light which reveals that we are children of God.

The journey to God does not have false starts and detours. Any road, any way of life, can be the starting point for the journey of faith. Even human sinfulness does not interrupt the journey, for sin becomes another ingredient within the journeying. Indeed, sinfulness often proves to be a remarkably significant element. Any road, any way of life, can provide the starting point for the journey of faith; any way can be special. Except for the times when we may be consciously resisting God by refusing to take responsibility for the freedom which God has given us, God is always creating us. Some succumb to discouragement over the way their lives have turned out. They wonder what good they have accomplished and doubt that God will be able to find in their lives any discernible pattern of holiness. But our worth, thankfully, does not depend upon how useful we have been to God's purposes or to our neighbor. To think that it does is to slide into the error which Paul had to combat among the Christians of his day, namely, to confuse righteousness with works. Each of us is the worst judge of precisely which activities or which stretches of our life were sufficiently centered upon God as to win our redemption. The failures, the discouragement and the frustrating struggles with our unruly nature which we would erase from the record—the things which we, unlike St. Paul, would certainly never boast about!—could well turn out to be the key elements of our personal creation.

What then does it mean to say that the life of the believer reveals the mystery of God?

Beneath all our conscious striving there unfolds an unconscious desire for God. As St. Augustine realized, even the tangling of that desire, which manifests itself as sin, testifies to the powerfully attractive reality of God. But to answer our question less abstractly, imagine some of the main chapters of any life story. Think of the maze of decisions, events and day-to-day encounters long since past. Think of the care involved in raising a family, or the hundreds of ways in which people have claimed our attention and our love. Think of all the moments of being in school, of work, of leisure, of caring for the needs of our bodies. As we recollect the years we have so far lived, the number and complexity of our activities, our intentions, our choices, and so forth, simply overwhelm the mind's efforts to grasp their inner relatedness and to determine what they add up to. The intricacy of any human life would by itself witness to the mystery of God. Who besides God could fathom and assay the worth of every breath we drew, every thought we entertained, every tear we shed, every sin we tried to bury, every regret we suffered, every triumph of patience, of compassion, of selfless care? In all of this the mystery of God must be revealed as the holy, silent and merciful presence which accompanies us throughout our lives. Whatever pattern or thread of meaning is found coursing through our lives is nothing other than the steady closeness of God. That alone does not change. That alone connects everything else.

How is the life of the believer a revelation of the mystery of God? We could answer this further by insisting that human living itself confirms the reality of God. Revelation, I have suggested, is the process of our coming out of hiding into the light of God's presence. And when we have done so, what is the outcome? What is a human being like who walks in the presence of God? No matter how disorganized or undirected that person's life appears to us, it can still illustrate a basic fidelity. The person can still believe that God has pressed a claim on his or her living and, despite personal waywardness, does not renounce that claim. Such a person remains a faithful witness to the unfailing closeness of God. Such a person proves this through the way he or she stands by commitments, through keeping confidences, and through staying close to family and friends. It is demonstrated by patience, by humble acceptance of limitations, and by trusting openness toward the future. God is revealed through the life of such a believer because we know that God is like that: God is faithful, God can be trusted, God cares and is patient, and God abides the limitations of human beings.

And then from the God-like qualities to the mystery: What makes a person lead such a life? Why does someone become and remain a disciple? Who raises up such people, and who sustains them? Why should goodness and compassion have triumphed in that person's life instead of greed and resentment? Why endure the process of being purged, or the battles with pride and stubbornness? Why does someone remain loyal to his or her word and honor the truth? Why weep for the hungry and the victims of misfortune? Why work for economic justice and actively oppose the arms race? Why be a peacemaker and practice true forgiveness? We are led, I suggest, into the scandal of goodness, of which the believer is the chief instance. Such scandal points the eyes of the rest of us in the direction of God. Drawn out of hiding and transparent because of the light of God's grace, the believer now reflects the glory of God—men and women fully alive, fully free.

By now the insight underlying the Dalai Lama's question to Thomas Merton should appear wonderfully correct. The vows point to what the religious person should be by life's end: someone truly and thoroughly poor, chaste and obedient. So too the promises taken by the Christian at baptism. What we profess, not only by assenting to the formula of the promises but also by consenting to the ritual washing, anointing and clothing, is our desire to be truly and thoroughly one with Christ in his dying and rising. What is expressed through the sacramental symbols is not just present fact, since upon leaving the church we still have much journeying to do; we belong to Christ but we have yet to put on the full implications of that belief. Rather, the sacramental ritual presupposes our hope that the God who has begun a good work in our lives will bring it to completion. When we have fully appropriated the mystery of our baptism, then our lives will properly be a revelation of the mystery of God.

FOOTNOTES

1. Michael Mott, *The Seven Mountains of Thomas Merton* (Boston: Houghton Mifflin Co., 1984), p. 548.

2. Hans Urs von Balthasar, *Origen: Spirit and Fire*, trans. Robert J. Daly, SJ (Washington, D.C.: Catholic University of America Press, 1984), p. 245.

3. John S. Dunne, *Reasons of the Heart: A Journey Into Solitude and Back Again Into the Human Circle* (Notre Dame, IN: University of Notre Dame Press, 1978).
   Sebastian Moore, *Let This Mind Be In You* (Minneapolis: Winston Press, 1985).

4. John Dominic Crossan, *In Parables: The Challenge of the Historical Jesus* (San Francisco: Harper & Row, 1973), pp. 45-52.

CHAPTER 5

Revelation and the Will of God

The People of God believes that it is led by the Spirit of the Lord, who fills the earth. Motivated by this faith, it labors to decipher authentic signs of God's presence and purpose in the happenings, needs, and desires in which this People has a part along with other people of our age. For faith throws a new light on everything.

—Vatican II, *The Pastoral Constitution on the Church in the Modern World*

Do not conform any longer to the pattern of this world, but be transformed by the renewing of your mind. Then you will be able to test and approve what God's will is—his good, pleasing and perfect will.

—Romans 12:2

*A*s we noted earlier, many Christians crave the miraculous. They would like God to give them some sign that would render their faith sure and their experience of God incontrovertible. For them revelation would be more appealing if it occurred graphically and compellingly, perhaps with an apparition, or a miracle, or some signal mutually agreed upon by God and the individual. A transfiguration episode (like in Mt 17:1-8), a healing when the medical world held no hope (like in Lk 8:43-48), the occurrence of something that only Christ could have known about, as when Jesus told Nathanael that he had seen him under the fig tree (Jn 1:48-50), Jesus' invitation to Thomas to touch the wound in his side (Jn 20:27-28)—if things like these happened to them, their faith would be much more secure. At least, so they think.

But revelation is not so interventionist as the biblical stories, or stories from the lives of the saints, might lead us to believe. Yes, God does give us signs, but even the signs God sends need to be

discerned and interpreted. Signs from God make no sense apart
from the faith that sees them as coming from the Lord. This is why
I have emphasized that ordinary experience, the situations of
everyday life, is the place where God meets us. To view the ordinary with eyes of faith is to begin to understand the mystery of
God's drawing near to us. As the Jesuit poet Gerard Manley
Hopkins wrote in *The Wreck of the Deutschland*: "For I greet him
the days I meet him, and bless when I understand."

What about the phrase *the will of God*? In the Our Father we
pray "thy will be done." Jesus, who said that only those who do the
Father's will shall enter the kingdom of heaven, prayed in much
the same way during his anguish in the garden: "Not what I will,
but what you will" (Mk 14:36). If doing the will of God is so
crucial to our salvation, shouldn't God have determined some
means by which human beings would know for certain what the
will of God for them was? Would it upset the ordinary running of
things for God to intervene directly and let us know what we are to
do if we want to be saved? Or would it be sufficient for us if Jesus,
the one who came not to do his own will but the will of the Father
who sent him, knew for certain what God expected of us and
communicated that message to his first disciples, and through them
to the church? Would the authority of the church be enough to
satisfy our craving for being sure about God's will in our regard?

We should not be misled by the portrait of Jesus given to us in
John's gospel. The Jesus who speaks there is the glorified Jesus, the
Jesus ever present to his beloved disciples. John reflects his community's experience of the Jesus who is present to them in their life
and in their prayer. During his own life Jesus set the example of a
person of faith:

> During the days of Jesus' life on earth, he offered up
> prayers and petitions with loud cries and tears to the one
> who could save him from death, and he was heard
> because of his reverent submission (Heb 5:7).

Jesus prayerfully had to discern what God's will for him meant. He
was tempted in the wilderness and there he discerned the Spirit's
way. He wrestled in the garden with the mystery and incomprehen-

sibility of the Father's way of liberating the world from its sin. The will of God did not fall from heaven into Jesus' head. He prayed for salvation from the power of death, just as we do, and "although he was a son, *he learned obedience* from what he suffered" (Heb 5:8, emphasis added). And we cannot take refuge in the church in order to bypass our own wrestling with the mystery of God or the hard way in which we too must learn reverent submission and obedience. Let me explain why.

Obedience and the Will of God

Many people draw a connection between the will of God and revelation without realizing it. Naturally we want to know what exactly God expects of us, what plan God has in store for us, what special project God might have designed for us to accomplish. But this is to get everything backward. By assuming that God has already planned our futures, we wind up trying to figure out what that picture is. In reality the figuring out itself—the discerning, the deciding, the taking responsibility for our own future—lies at the heart of every spiritual journey. God will not intervene in our lives and declare to us, so loudly and clearly that we shall never doubt it, what we are to do. Failing this, we should not go looking for the second-best route and ask the church, or some human agent, to tell us infallibly how we are to live and act, what we are to do or to think.

The meaning of religious obedience is not a matter which only concerns Christians who have joined religious communities. Religious obedience, properly understood, pertains more broadly to Christian existence in general. How does each of us come to know God's will, and what does it mean to obey it? In order to answer this I must first explain the dynamic relationship between call and desire, or between divine initiative and human response. This is the foundation in terms of which religious obedience—and the response of every Christian to the will of God—needs to be understood.

First, a general observation about religious obedience. For the most part the obedience which governs the lives of men and women in religious communities is practical or pragmatic. Obedience ensures the smooth and efficient running of communities and apostolates; it frees individuals from becoming enmeshed in those details of common life and common work which need not properly be their concern. A parallel could be drawn here with the life of any one of us in the church, for the church informs us about how the practicing Catholic ought to live, to behave, and even on occasion to think. In fact life in any human community, religious or otherwise, requires some measure of obedience for the smooth and effective running of things.

Sometimes religious people are further instructed to regard the decisions of their superiors, or the deliberations of their communities, as coming from the Lord. This now is more than the pragmatic side of obedience. To say that a decision "comes from the Lord" is to appeal to a person's faith. There is something profoundly true about this, because deliberations carried on in the Spirit of Jesus might very well be prompted by the risen Lord. However, I should qualify this by adding that, theologically speaking, no one can directly represent Christ for another. One text frequently appealed to by religious authorities is "He who listens to you listens to me" (Lk 10:16). But this saying occurs in a passage where Jesus is preparing his disciples as they undertake the mission on which he is sending them. They are to speak and act in his name. Whatever is done to the disciples is also done to Jesus, just as those who reject Jesus will also be rejecting the Father who sent him. And yet the disciple does not simply substitute for Jesus, anymore than Jesus, who speaks the Father's words, directly and immediately substitutes for the Father. For the whole point of the disciple's preaching and witnessing is to enable others to enter into a faith relationship with Christ. Like John the Baptist pointing to Jesus, the disciple eventually has to declare, "This is the one I meant" (Jn 1:30).

No doubt the idea that a religious superior or church leader actually stands in place of Christ well might contribute to a person's motivation for listening to and obeying another Christian. But the grounds for obedience should not be confused with the motivation which supports it.

For the most part, it seems to me, the notion of religious

obedience has been founded upon the belief that God's will can be signified by one person to another, or by a community to its members. The divine will, it is supposed, receives expression in a community's constitutions, rules and deliberations, as well as in relevant church documents and papal teaching. Of course if the will of God finds expression there, it is surely signified for all Christians in the New Testament writings and, some people would urge, by the teaching authority of the church. The basis for this supposition is the church's conviction of Jesus' abiding presence among his followers through the gift of the Spirit. The Spirit of Jesus resides actively in the minds and hearts of his disciples, particularly where two or three gather prayerfully in his name. In prayer the disciples can turn to Jesus for support and guidance, asking him to help them to decide what course of action will best promote the glory of God. In other words, religious obedience builds upon the premise of faith that the Holy Spirit will guide a community of believers.

Permit me to register two points here. First, the notion of the will of God should not be extended too facilely to embrace all the particulars of a person's life. We learn to find God *in* the many details of our lives, but it does not follow that all the specific events and circumstances of our lives are the result of God's will for us. Some people respond to everything in life by saying, "It is God's will." On the one hand such a response can stem from a terrible misinterpretation of Christian resignation, and it fosters a form of spirituality which is much too passive. On the other hand such a response could also be that of someone who is far too eager to find the hand of God in everything, even in all the incidental details of life. God does not will electrical power failures, the winning of a football game, the rain that spoils a picnic, and so on. This type of spirituality is far too undiscriminating.

Religious obedience has to steer a course between an attitude which is excessively passive in the matter of seeking and following the divine will, and one that is overly eager in spotting and celebrating the divine will. Neither a community's constitutions nor papal or episcopal teaching can be equated with divine revelation, even when certain church teachings are proposed infallibly.

For strictly speaking, as we have seen, revelation does not consist of
written statements about God. Revelation refers to the process of
God's self-communication to human beings:

> The term "revelation" has both a general and a strict
> sense. It has been applied to the constant evidence
> which God provides of Himself "in created realities."
> This manifestation of God is available to all human
> beings, even in the present condition of the human
> race. Strictly speaking, however, revelation designates
> the communication of God which is in no way deserved
> by us, for it has as its aim our participation in the life of
> the Trinity, a share in divine life itself. This revelation is
> a gift of God upon which no one has a claim. Because it
> goes beyond anything which we can dare imagine, the
> proper response to this revelation is that self-surrender
> known as the obedience of faith.[1]

Or, as I have been suggesting, revelation might also be viewed as
God's uncovering us and drawing us into the freedom and trust
which belong to the children of God. The writings, teachings and
official documents of a religious community or of the church itself
reflect the confluence of many human factors. Grace does, of
course, intersect the human story at many points, but grace never
so overtakes this story—which also includes the process of revelation and the writing of scripture—that it overrides the human
element. After all, it is human beings who compose rules, make
laws, discern and implement apostolic goals and projects, yet these
features of religious life can vary considerably, depending on
historical periods, cultures and specific religious charisms. Thus,
although religious rules have sometimes in the past been proposed
as expressions of God's will, they never actually coincided with
some absolutely clear and definitive divine plan or idea.

The will of God is not discovered like a treasure buried in a
field; it is not some secret divine thought awaiting to be unearthed
either in prayer or through the command of someone in authority,
not even if that someone happened to be an apostle. As disciples
of Jesus, we believe that the will of God is manifested to us *through*
the gospel, *through* the words and example of Jesus, *through* the

ideals of the kingdom of God which Jesus proclaimed. The Christ-event, after all, constitutes a unique moment of God's self-communication. But the application of the ideals and values of the gospel to any particular life-situation is a matter of personal prayer and discernment. The need to be ever reading and interpreting the gospels, to be ever attentive to the word of God however that word comes to us, draws us to notice again the event-character of revelation. What God actually wants of us is something which each of us must determine for ourselves. We can never escape taking full responsibility for this. Consequently, our obedience can only be *directly* given to God. With respect to the will of God, therefore, we might say that the divine will is general rather than specific. God wills that we seek the kingdom of God and God's justice, that we follow and imitate Jesus, that we allow God's redeeming love to bring us into the freedom of the children of God. We affirm these things, obviously, as men and women who have already encountered Christ.

This brings us to the second point. Given the number of different situations in which we might find ourselves throughout the course of our lives, it is conceivable that any one of them could be a place which realizes God's will for us. As men and women of faith, we learn to surrender our futures to God in much the same way that biblical figures of faith like Abraham, Moses, Mary or Jesus opened their futures to God. People can externalize their interior surrender by promising obedience to one of their brothers or sisters. This obedience sacramentalizes, as it were, their response to that inner mystery of grace which draws all of us to itself.

But there is something else to consider. Every situation contains the possibility of our discovering within it God's involvement with the world here and now. Every situation of our lives, even that particular form of personal sinfulness which belongs to each of us, is a place where God's grace attracts and meets us. We should not think that the will of God means, concretely, that there is one definite, special thing God wishes us to do. Not only is there no possibility of jumping inside the mind of God, but we ought not to think that God thinks, plans and wills the way we do. Because so

few of us ever know ourselves honestly and thoroughly, and because
we labor under psychological and spiritual conditions which often
prevent our making fully informed and free decisions, we can do no
more from a human point of view than to seek God's glory. We
simply follow Jesus in the hope that we have done the best we can
in searching for and finding the will of God. God wills that we
should take seeking the kingdom of God in our lives seriously. God
wills that we should become men and women of faith and love.
God wills—it is God's glory—that we should be people who are
fully human and fully free. The quest for God's will, therefore, does
not conclude in the certitude of religious authority assuring us that
we are doing what God wants, but in the conviction of a faith
continually reaching out to God. Prayerful discernment is not a
process of figuring out the hidden designs of God, any more than
the process of revelation is actually a matter of divine secrets
coming to light. Now, since that is the case, and since we are all
called upon to love God, what prevents us from demonstrating that
love by freely and sincerely obeying another, particularly when such
obedience allows us to express our readiness to hear the word of
God and keep it? In short, it makes sense for disciples to practice
religious obedience, that is, to demonstrate in their lives reverent
submission to the Spirit of Jesus. But they should not mythologize
the will of God.

A further point. Because it is always possible to find God in
other situations, seeking the Lord will have to be a permanent
feature of Christian living. Like merchants on the lookout for fine
pearls, we must always be searching for God. From a theological
point of view, the divine plan for the world is realized every time
men and women allow themselves to be drawn by their deepest
desires for God: their longing for union, their thirst for justice and
peace, their desire for community. Theologically speaking every
situation in which truly believing people find themselves is a
providential setting; that situation becomes the place where
revelation occurs.

As followers of Jesus who are trying to practice obedience we
can say, therefore, that we are where God wants us to be. But we
must add that God also expects us to be looking for the divine

presence tomorrow, since there is no human situation in which grace has reached a standstill. A young person who is considering whether to marry or to join a religious community has no way of knowing with absolute certitude which state of life God wants him or her to embrace any more than one could infallibly declare that God intended someone to be a doctor, a diplomat, a corporate executive or a cleric. From experience we know that there are attractions on both sides of the marriage-celibacy line. If the person elects to marry, we ought not to conclude that marriage is now God's will for that individual, as if from all eternity God had decreed that the individual should marry. In a contingent universe matters could always have been otherwise. If a person believes that God's will pre-determines the shape of his or her earthly pilgrimage, then that individual will spend life in the clouded, unsure state of a faith which is frustrating and confining rather than energizing and liberating. Discernment is not a matter of figuring out what is on God's mind.

There is no means of second-guessing the divine will because there is no plan for each and every life which God has worked out in advance, as it were. To think or speak this way is to introduce temporality into God and to misunderstand how our personal creation occurs. God stands above time, for God is everlastingly present, and the world with all that is in it remains eternally present to God. To use a spatial metaphor, perhaps we could say that divine grace is not so much behind us, pushing us through life according to a pre-established history as it is above us and ahead of us, coming to us from the future. We have desires and we make choices. We respond in faith, from that measure of freedom we have been able to realize, to the overtures of grace. In short, most of the time Christians obey those who exercise religious authority for quite practical reasons. But their obedience in some situations also reflects a deep belief that they are always, day by day, responding to God out of faith. Their decision to obey another externalizes a way of being both human and religious. We have no unquestionable guarantee that what a superior commands is in fact God's will, any more than we can be sure that the decision to embrace a particular way of life in the first place manifested what God has willed for us. The will of God applies generally, not specifically.

I repeat: The issue is not one of attempting to guess what is on the divine mind for us to do. The point is that any number of situations can be the providential settings in which one serves and glorifies God. As men and women of God, we are willing to trust that if the community or its superior wishes us to engage in a particular work, then that work *may* express what God wants for us. That is, it can be the place where divine grace fruitfully and victoriously intersects the future which we desire to surrender to God. Something similar, I should think, would also hold true for parishes, or diocesan assemblies, Christian families or any gathering of those who claim to be followers of Jesus. The experience of religious communities has much to offer the church, for they provide a model of discernment, concrete instances of men and women prayerfully seeking together what the Spirit intends for them. While no one wants to prejudice the proper and legitimate functioning of authority, nothing is accomplished when we insist that the church is a community of disciples and then carry on as if the experience and desires of the community can be discounted by those who exercise authority within it.

Mission and the Will of God

One of the chief factors contributing to a kind of mission myth is the belief that Jesus received his mission from the Father in a way that spared him both the uncertainty of faith and the risk of hope. As a consequence of this misunderstanding, some Christians think that the individual believer is spared any future faith struggle whenever ecclesiastical or religious authorities have spoken. Judging from the gospel accounts, however, it seems unlikely that God ever spoke to Jesus so authoritatively and unambiguously that Jesus no longer had to pray, to discern, to take stock of his labors on behalf of the kingdom, or to look toward the future with confidence in the ultimate triumph of grace. There is nothing magical about religious call and mission, neither in Jesus' case nor in ours. Call and mission arise, of course, within the mystery of God's dealings with human beings who have learned how to listen to God's word.

But the authority which grounds our response to that word ought not to be identified with the voice of the church or of a religious community speaking on behalf of God. What grounds our response is an intense desire to *be* for and to *live* for God.

To be on a mission is just another way of stating that one has been sent. The basic Christian model of mission is, of necessity, Jesus, the one who was sent into the world by the Father. The particular mission upon which a religious person has embarked can only be an inadequate realization here and now of the much more basic fact that in his or her very being he or she has been called by God. *This applies to every Christian.* The spiritual vision which sustains us never coincides totally with the specific circumstances in which we find ourselves. This excess of vision over concrete situation leads to what St. Ignatius Loyola called the "magis," that apostolic "more" which leaves a person wondering what else he or she might do for the sake of Jesus and the kingdom.

People of faith are those who believe that ultimately God alone can "call" a person (and I am using the word *call* metaphorically). They further believe that the God who has been revealed to us as the Father of Jesus Christ has called them to be disciples and companions of Jesus. They believe even more concretely and profoundly that Jesus has missioned them to a particular way of life and service in the modern world. "Calling the Twelve to him," Mark wrote, "he sent them out two by two" (Mk 6:7). In other words, being with Jesus entails being sent to proclaim and to teach the gospel.

Now, what I am interested in here is not the mission to a specific place or work, or to a particular form of Christian commitment, whether within marriage, religious community, priesthood or the single state. This is an important though secondary aspect to the notion of religious call. What is of primary importance is the conviction that God has pressed a claim upon our life. This conviction is integrated into our religious consciousness. It confers meaningfulness and purpose upon our life and work, and it enables us to discover that we have a definite place within the broader scheme of divine providence. Our belief that God has called us to be people of faith, to be Christian and to be companions of Jesus, contributes to a basic vision out of which we interpret our own personal history and the history of the human race.

But call can only be understood with reference to a corresponding desire, for the sense of being called is the reverse side of a desire both to do something absolutely worthwhile with our life and to have someone tell us, definitively and unambiguously, that our life has ultimate and lasting worth. Since no human being can unconditionally guarantee for another that what she or he has done (or is about to do) has furthered (or will further) God's saving plans for the world, religious people accept the particular situation of their living *in the hope* that those things to which they have now dedicated their lives will actually contribute to God's greater glory.

The critical importance of this hope should not be overlooked. Every specific mission, each particular work in which the disciples of Jesus are engaged, is a lived expression of the theological virtue of hope. Paul writes: "And we know that in all things God works for the good of those who love him, who have been called according to his purpose" (Rom 8:28). Mission and hope are inseparable, for the outcome of every work which advances the reign of God in human hearts depends completely on God. That outcome is often hidden from the eyes of the ones whom God has called to live and labor in the company of Jesus. The connection between mission and hope also obtained for Jesus. He died without seeing what kind of yield would be harvested from the labors of his mission to preach the reign of God. In fact, the cross of Jesus is the chief Christian sign of hope; that is, the cross calls attention to the hope of him who laid down his life for our sake. Jesus had nothing to rely on except God's word, which he too heard in faith, that God's designs upon his life would be accomplished. Like us, Jesus also had to trust that "in all things God works for the good of those who love him."

Where then does that leave us? That leaves us with the fundamental human desire which all of us share to devote our lives—our energies, our minds and affections, our talents and imaginations—to praising and serving the holy mystery which is God. Only that holy mystery warrants such a total self-gift of the human person. In other words, God alone can be loved and served with all our heart, with all our soul, with all our mind, and with all of our strength. Furthermore, only the holy mystery of God, which the Christian knows to be the Father of our Lord Jesus Christ, can guarantee that a person's commitment in faith to Jesus makes his or her human existence worthwhile.

The key here is desire. A man or a woman has to want more than anything else to be for and to live for God. Desires themselves are signs of grace. The configuration of our desires reveals the pattern of grace which God has been creating in our lives. Desire provides a measure of how deeply we feel called by God to serve Christ and his church; the intensity of our desire indicates how strongly and gladly we will be able to respond to the attractiveness of Jesus and the ideals of God's kingdom. Call and desire are correlative. We cannot be called to something we do not want. The Christian sense of mission is a matter of perceiving that we have been called by God, but it is also a matter of having experienced that our deepest desire is to be for, to live for, and to die for the God who has come close to us in the person of Jesus.

Perhaps we should understand the mission of Jesus—his being sent "into the world"—in much the same way. For Jesus was also called. The dimensions of that call were shaped by his own faith and by his knowledge of the God who had in times past called the prophets to speak the divine word to Israel. But Jesus was also a man with intense desire: to do the Father's will, to forgive sins and proclaim the nearness of God, to seek the Father's glory in all things. Jesus' sense of being sent governed everything he did and all that he was. Jesus could not have been called to something he did not want, any more than we could. If Paul, for example, had not wanted to serve the God of his ancestors so zealously, he would not have been ready to hear, let alone respond to Jesus' call on the Damascus road.

It often happens that people wind up doing things for Jesus' sake which they do not find particularly attractive, but they do so precisely because at a deeper level of their being they want to be for and live for God. They do so because they want to be wherever they perceive Jesus is, even if Jesus should lead them by way of the cross. In the case of Jesus, we might say that he wanted to be wherever he believed the Father was leading him. And the Father was the one who guaranteed the absolute worth of Jesus' mission: "You are my Son, whom I love; with you I am well pleased" (Mk 1:11).

It goes without saying that the sense of mission belongs to every Christian because each of us is a man or woman who has been sent into the world. Nevertheless, the prominence given to this element of gospel spirituality by many Christians suggests that the religious person ought to be one who feels a certain urgency about life, who experiences a strong desire to help others to know God, and whose basic desire for God has translated itself into a desire to be with Jesus. Paul is a good example of such a person: "*I want to know Christ* and the power of his resurrection and the fellowship of sharing in his sufferings, becoming like him in his death" (Phil 3:10, emphasis added). But it was Jesus who provided the model of someone who has experienced the urgency which underlies desire and mission: "I have come to bring fire on the earth, and how I wish it were already kindled! But I have a baptism to undergo, and how distressed I am until it is completed!" (Lk 12:49-50).

FOOTNOTES

1. *Sharing the Light of Faith*: The National Catechetical Directory for Catholics of the United States (Washington, D.C.: United States Catholic Conference, 1979), no. 49.

"If, while we seek to be justified in Christ, it becomes
evident that we ourselves are sinners, does that mean
that Christ promotes sin? Absolutely not! If I rebuild
what I destroyed, I prove that I am a lawbreaker. For
through the law I died to the law so that I might live
for God. I have been crucified with Christ and I no
longer live, but Christ lives in me. The life I live in
the body, I live by faith in the Son of God, who loved
me and gave himself for me. I do not set aside the
grace of God, for if righteousness could be gained
through the law, Christ died for nothing!"

—Galatians 2:17-21

*T*his passage from Paul's Letter to the Galatians contains
many of the ideas we have been discussing. This will
become clear, if the reader permits me to offer the following
paraphrase:

If it becomes evident to us, in the course of our efforts
to be disciples of Jesus, just how much of us has still to
be redeemed, still to be created, still to be brought out
of hiding, does that mean that Jesus is trying to humili-
ate us by showing us how incomplete we are? Of course
not. For consider: If we set about repairing something we
broke, then everyone knows—we are implicitly admitting
the fact—that we are people who break things. Well, the
wisdom of this world can bring us just so far in our
attempts to become fully human. We do, after all, find it
difficult to do what is right, to be all that we are capable
of being. One thing is certain, however: We cannot
redeem ourselves, fashion ourselves according to God's
image, without help. We are sinful people, ever trying to
restore what we've broken.

But we have been crucified with Christ, and so now
a new life pulsates within us, the life of Jesus, our risen
Lord. That life is God's own, a life to which we have

135

access only by faith. And what is the content of this
faith? What do we believe in so strongly? We believe in
the incomprehensible love of God, a love so great that
only the crucified Jesus is a word and deed powerful
enough to convince us of this truth. God's love for us is
pure and utter gift. If we could be fully created in any
other way than by joining ourselves to Jesus in his dying
and rising, if we could make it on our own, equipped
with all the wisdom this world has to offer, then the
death of Jesus was a waste of God's time.

I do not pretend that this rendering of the text does full justice
to all the issues Paul is addressing in his letter to the Galatian
Christians, but I hope it conveys some of the intention underlying
his thinking. At least it helps to summarize many of the ideas
raised throughout these chapters. I have been talking about revelation—the great mystery of Christ in us, our hope of glory—in terms
of spirituality, that is, from within our experience of God, the One
who draws all things out of hiding into God's own liberating,
creative light.

I think it can be said that the notion of revelation subsumes, in
one way or another, all the other aspects of Christian belief. After
reflecting on the significance of Adam's trying to steal away from
God's attention, we looked at the church's sacramental life for
examples of how God uncovers for us the major moments in the
process of our ongoing creation. To participate in the life of the
people of God is to be steadily uncovered—created and redeemed—
by the Spirit of Jesus.

Mind and heart together have their parts to play as God's
revealing action unfolds. God does not come to the human scene
from some place beyond and outside our world. God is already
within the human situation, inside the workings of our minds and
hearts. All subsequent reflection about God begins from within
some experience of God, and we looked at three situations of
being-in-faith: the experience of the prophet, of the pilgrim, and of
the lover. There are other aspects of Christian religious experience,
to be sure, and thus it was important to think about how the

religious experience of the disciples had been shaped by their being-with-Jesus. We discussed twelve aspects of that experience, and then remarked on the way our sense of sin and forgiveness changes as our discipleship deepens and grows.

Next, we looked at the life of the believer in the various dimensions of his or her struggle with grace, since only there, if anywhere, is the mystery of God—Christ in us, our hope of glory— revealed. All are called to perfection, Vatican II reminds us, but the triumph of our creation will not come until we are definitively joined to God forever. Sin and temporary losses of direction should never discourage us. Finally we reflected on the connection be- tween revelation and God's will. The will of God is not revealed to us in the dramatic ways in which one might imagine God speaking to the prophets of old, or to Abraham and Moses, or even to the seer of the Book of Revelation. The will of God cannot be told to us by another person, certainly not with an absolute assuredness that reaches into the particulars of our lives. What God wants of us is revealed only as we learn to live in the freedom and light of the divine presence. The will of God for us unfolds as we follow Jesus, as we listen to him and watch him in the gospel scenes, and as we constantly attend to the direction he takes as he walks ahead of us. To become obedient is to live a life of trusting surrender to the holy mystery of God. Adam ran away from that kind of life. Jesus, the new Adam, embraced it. The Adam in us keeps running away, but the Christ-self knows better. And herein lies the source of much of our spiritual struggle and growth. Here lies the taproot of Christian spirituality.

Is it not better to have met Jesus than to have continued blissfully unaware of the great potential which is ours? Is it not better to have been drawn out of hiding than to have spent our lives dodging the light of self-knowledge and God's purifying love? Is it not better to be free with Jesus than to have remained ever vulnerable to the many fears which make human beings easy targets for everything which would dehumanize them, making them less alive and free, less men and women *of God*? Isn't it better to have met Jesus in the church than to have passed our lives caged in by the very occasions in life which ought to have fed our hopes and our faith? For God did not bring us into the company of Jesus in order to cripple our spontaneity or to make us doubt the possibility of our ever being fully human. God brought us to Jesus—to his church—in order to learn, and to touch, the holy mystery which is God's life-giving presence.